First World War
and Army of Occupation
War Diary
France, Belgium and Germany

25 DIVISION
Divisional Troops
112 Brigade Royal Field Artillery
1 September 1915 - 28 February 1919

WO95/2234/1

The Naval & Military Press Ltd
www.nmarchive.com
Published in association with The National Archives

Published by

The Naval & Military Press Ltd

Unit 10 Ridgewood Industrial Park,

Uckfield, East Sussex,

TN22 5QE England

Tel: +44 (0) 1825 749494

www.naval-military-press.com

www.nmarchive.com

This diary has been reprinted in facsimile from the original. Any imperfections are inevitably reproduced and the quality may fall short of modern type and cartographic standards.

© **Crown Copyright**
Images reproduced by permission of The National Archives, London, England, 2015.

Contents

Document type	Place/Title	Date From	Date To
Heading	WO95/2234 112 Brigade Royal Field Artily		
Heading	112th Brigade R.F.A. Sep 1915-Feb 1919		
Heading	25th Division 112th Bde R.F.A. Vol I		
War Diary	Leipzic Barracks. Aldershot.	01/09/1915	26/09/1915
War Diary	Southampton	26/09/1915	26/09/1915
War Diary	Le Havre	27/09/1915	28/09/1915
War Diary	Caestre	29/09/1915	29/09/1915
War Diary	Pradelles	30/09/1915	30/09/1915
War Diary	Le Bizet.	01/10/1915	06/10/1915
War Diary	Lebbizet.	08/10/1915	10/10/1915
War Diary	Le Bizet	11/10/1915	31/10/1915
Heading	25th Division Nov 15 112th Bde RFA Vol 2		
War Diary	Le Bizet.	01/11/1915	30/11/1915
Heading	25th Div 112th Bde Rfa Vol 3		
War Diary	Le Bizet.	01/12/1915	31/12/1915
Miscellaneous	Report of 112th Brigade. R.F.A. Night		
Miscellaneous	Supplementary Report of the Minor Operation of the night	28/12/1915	28/12/1915
Heading	112th Brigade R.F.A. 25th Divisional Artillery January 1916.		
Heading	112 R.F.A. 25th Div Vol 4		
War Diary	Le Bizet.	01/01/1916	26/01/1916
War Diary	Caestre Area	27/01/1916	27/01/1916
Heading	112th. Brigade R.F.A. 25th Divisional Artillery		
War Diary	La Brearde	01/02/1916	10/03/1916
War Diary	Berguette.	11/03/1916	12/03/1916
War Diary	Averdoingt.	13/03/1916	31/03/1916
Heading	112th Brigade R.F.A. 25th Divisional Artillery April 1916		
War Diary	Averdoingt	01/04/1916	03/04/1916
War Diary	Neuville Au Cornet.	04/04/1916	06/04/1916
War Diary	Mont St Eloi.	07/04/1916	07/04/1916
War Diary	Villers Au Bois.	05/04/1916	25/04/1916
War Diary	In The Field Villers Au Bois	25/04/1916	27/04/1916
War Diary	In The Field	28/04/1916	30/04/1916
Heading	112th. Brigade R.F.A. 25th Divisional Artillery May 1916.		
War Diary	In The Field	01/05/1916	31/05/1916
Heading	112th Brigade R.F.A. 25th Divisional Artillery June 1916.		
War Diary	St Michel	01/06/1916	15/06/1916
War Diary	Occoches	16/06/1916	17/06/1916
War Diary	Montrelet	18/06/1916	28/06/1916
War Diary	Harponville	29/06/1916	30/06/1916
Heading	War Diary Headquarters. 112th Brigade, R.F.A. July 1916		
War Diary	Harponville	01/07/1916	01/07/1916
War Diary	Vadencourt	02/07/1916	05/07/1916
War Diary	In The Field	06/07/1916	31/07/1916
Heading	112th Brigade. Royal Field Artillery. August 1916		

War Diary	In The Field.	01/08/1916	31/08/1916
Heading	112th Brigade R.F.A. 25th. Divisional Artillery September 1916.		
War Diary	In The Field.	01/09/1916	30/09/1916
Heading	112th Brigade R.F.A. 25th Divisional Artillery October 1916		
War Diary	In The Field	01/10/1916	31/10/1916
Heading	112th. Brigade R.F.A. 25th Divisional Artillery November 1916.		
War Diary	In The Field Sheet 57 DSE R 33 d 2.5.	01/11/1916	30/11/1916
Heading	112th. Brigade R.F.A. 25th. Divisional Artillery December 1916.		
War Diary	In The Field.	01/12/1916	28/02/1917
Heading	112th Brigade Royal Field Artillery March 1918		
War Diary	In The Field	01/03/1918	31/03/1918
Heading	112th Brigade Royal Field Artillery April 1918		
War Diary	In The Field	01/04/1918	31/01/1919
War Diary	Carnieres Nord	01/02/1919	28/02/1919

WO/95/2234

/1 112 Brigade Royal Field
Artillery

25TH DIVISION
DIVL ARTILLERY

112TH BRIGADE R.F.A.
SEP 1915- FEB 1919

Diary for July 1917 missing

121/7594

25th Kmun

112th Bde: R.F.A.
Vol: I

Sept & Oct 15

Dec 19

Army Form C.2118

WAR DIARY
or
INTELLIGENCE SUMMARY

(Erase heading not required.)

Instructions regarding War Diaries and Intelligence Summaries are contained in F.S. Regs., Part II. and the Staff Manual respectively. Title Pages will be prepared in manuscript.

Place	Date	Hour	Summary of Events and Information	Remarks and references to Appendices
LEIPZIC BARRACKS. ALDERSHOT.	1/9/15.		Brigade in Training.	
	26/9/15.	12.mdt. to 5.am.	Brigade started in 11 trains for foreign service.	
SOUTHAMPTON.		8.a.m.	Brigade Headquarters entrained for foreign service. More explicit directions regarding necessity for immediately watering horses should be given.	
		5.pm.	Sailed.	
LE HAVRE	27/9/15.	9.a.m.	Disembarkation began.	
		4.pm.	Disembarkation completed.	
		5.pm.	Entrainment began in 5 Trains.	
	28/9/15.	5.am.	Entrainment ended. Arrangements for hot water for men might be more frequent	
CAESTRE.	29/9/15.	1.am.	Detrainment began. All the way numerous halts, but at only 3 regular places	
		11.am.	Detrainment ended. No arrangements for billets made. Made our own in area ordered.	
PRADELLES.		1.p.m.	Brigade concentrated. Firing heard in distance to eastward.	
"	30./9/15.	7-30 am.	Marched off with Battery Staffs, (Authority 2nd Army Corps), and reported to C.R.A. 25th Divisional Artillery.	

[signature]
LT. COL., R.F.A.
COMMANDING 112th BRIGADE R.F.A.

Army Form C. 2118

WAR DIARY or INTELLIGENCE SUMMARY

(Erase heading not required.)

Instructions regarding War Diaries and Intelligence Summaries are contained in F. S. Regs, Part II and the Staff Manual respectively. Title Pages will be prepared in manuscript.

Place	Date	Hour	Summary of Events and Information	Remarks and references to Appendices
LE BIZET.	30.9.15.	7. p.m.	Batteries joined and went into position. A/112. 1 Section. B/112. 1 Section. C/112. D/112. under orders of 50th Divisional Artillery. 1 Section of B/112 joined Headquarters	
	1/10/15.	7. p.m.	1 Section of A/112 joined Headquarters. No. of rounds fired, 3794.	
	2/10/15		In defence of trenches 90 to 101. Details in daily reports attached, under orders of C.R.A. 50th Division, temporarily. Zones of fire 90 to 94. A/112. 92 to 94. C/112. 95 to 101. D/112. 99 to 101. B/112.	
			Night Lines. A/112. B/112. C/112. D/112.	
			No.1.Gun. C.16.B.9.6. No.1.Gun. C.4.b.3.1. No.1.Gun. C.10.b.8.3. No.1.Gun. C.4.d.4.4.	
			No.2.Gun. C.11.c.4.7. No.2.Gun.) No.2.Gun. C.10.b.7.5. No.2.Gun. C.4.d.3.7.	
			No.3.Gun. C.10.b.8.5.)c.4.b.1.1. No.3.Gun. C.10.b.6.8. No.3.Gun. C.4.d.0.9.	
			No.4.Gun. C.4.d.7.3. No.3.Gun.) No.4.Gun. C.4.d.4.3. No.4.Gun. C.4.a.9.1.	
			No.4.Gun. C.4.b.0.2.	
			No. of rounds fired. 126/A.	
	3/10/15.	Mdt.	Covering trenches 90 to 101 as on 2nd October in support of 151st Brigade. No. of Rounds, fired, 108/A. Details in daily reports attached.	
		3-30- p.m	Command taken over by 25th Division.	
		7-30. p.m.	In support of 74th Infantry Brigade in same position and same task. Authority. B.M. 25th Divisional Artillery. 45. (G.S.O. 25th Division. 19.G.). 3.10.15. Reported to B.M. 74th Infantry Brigade, through C.B.R. by telephone.	
		7-15	O.Cs. of 13th Cheshires and 11th Lancs Fusiliers ordered to communicate with 112th Brigade.	

Army Form C. 21

WAR DIARY
or
INTELLIGENCE SUMMARY
(Erase heading not required.)

Instructions regarding War Diaries and Intelligence Summaries are contained in F. S. Regs., Part II. and the Staff Manual respectively. Title Pages will be prepared in manuscript.

Place	Date	Hour	Summary of Events and Information	Remarks and references to Appendices
LE BIZET.	4/10/15		Covering trenches 90 to 101. No. of rounds fired. 137/A.	
		6.a.m.	Enemy fired on trenches and houses with .77mm guns about 32 rounds.	
		12. noon	Hostile aeroplane passed over: appeared armoured against bullets. Details as in attached reports.	
	5/10/15.	11am. to 12. noon	Covering trenches 90 to 101. No. of rounds fired. 182/A Some rounds 77.m.m. on trenches. Weather hazy and rainy.	
		5.a.m.	Good results on enemy's trenches fired 16 rounds gun fire: one round struck metal, and there was a big flash.	
		8.a.m. to 2.p.m.	Registration and good results on fire trenches and a BLANCHISERIE.	
		8.p.m.	Fire on Hostile working party.	
		11.a.m.	Retaliation on 77.m.m. Gun which was shelling trenches.	
		10-30 a.m.	Enemies Troops about 10 men observed in dirty white uniform carrying loads suspended on poles about 8 feet long. The loads were black. They were observed entering communication trenches and proceeding towards the front. Details on attached reports.	

Army Form C. 2118

WAR DIARY
or
INTELLIGENCE SUMMARY
(Erase heading not required.)

Instructions regarding War Diaries and Intelligence Summaries are contained in F. S. Regs., Part II. and the Staff Manual respectively. Title Pages will be prepared in manuscript.

Place	Date	Hour	Summary of Events and Information	Remarks and references to Appendices
LE BIZET.	6/10/15.	4-45. am	Covering Trenches 90 to 101. No of rounds fired. 79/A	
			Six rounds over 92 trench as test.	
		10-30 am.	Retaliation & Registration and tests especially near BLANCHISSERIE to C/112. D/112 reported communications bad. Since entering this locality there has been much difficulty with all the communications. The wires have been too numerous, and have been laid so as to get induction. Much labour has been undertaken by Lieut. Carr, and telephonists, and now	
		to 7. p.m.	the telephone service is improving a little.	
		3-45 p.m.	Good results on parapet by A/112.	
		4-15.a.m. to 10-35	Guns in action at the VATS near BRASSERIE on LYS.	
		1-15 p.m.	Machine Gun emplacement by D/112.	
			Covering Trenches 90 to 101. No of rounds fired 41/A Registration and retaliation. Weather bright.	
		2.a.m.	The two telephonists were disturbed by someone round Brigade Headquarters billet. They chased him and 1 man Gunner MANNING F. No.71840. was fired at and wounded in the leg. He replied but no result was discovered.	
		11. a.m.	Bursts of Hostile fire 30 rounds T.S. and 9. H.E. unaimed searching fire. Fuzes dug out	
		12.30 p.m.	without time rings. Direction from East.	
		11. am.	On 77.m.m. Battery Near C.17.a.2.8. by A/112.	
		12-30 p.m.	Other Batteries on trenches 1st line by C. & D.	
		4-30. to	On enemys trenches.	
		6.p.m.	B/112 on Machine Gun on call from Infantry.	
		10.pm.	The wire spikes with loops in rear of enemys' trenches have been wired up. Authority B/112. 1. Round from A/112.	

Army Form C. 2118

WAR DIARY
or
INTELLIGENCE SUMMARY
(Erase heading not required.)

Instructions regarding War Diaries and Intelligence Summaries are contained in F.S. Regs., Part II. and the Staff Manual respectively. Title Pages will be prepared in manuscript.

Place	Date	Hour	Summary of Events and Information	Remarks and references to Appendices
LEBBIZET.	8/10/15	11-45	Covering trenches 90 to 101	
			No. of rounds fired 61/A Hostile fire Nil.	
			Weather very dull.	
		10.am.	Registration at D/112 at BLANCHISSERIE.	
		6-30. am.	Machine Gun emplacement by D/112. Infantry call.	
			Enemy's trenches by B/112. ditto.	
		5. pm.	1 test round A/112.	
		5-30. p.m.	Section 1st line G. trench registration.	
		12.33	On a report that C/113 had killed 2 of the Lancashire Fusiliers telephoned up by Captain Barker I stopped firing of the Batteries 112th Brigade, and checked their fire. I also sent Lieut Carr, orderly officer to C/113 to stop them. This officer had previously got a message by telephone through to O.C. 113th Brigade to stop, C/113.	
	9/10/15.	12-30 p.m.	Covering trenches 90 to 101. Rounds fired 97/A/ Hostile fire Nil.	
			Sand Bags redoubt damaged C.10.b.5.5. 14 direct hits very successful; set on fire by A/112.	
		3-30.	Working Parties C/112 & D/112 (opposite trench 98-97)	
		5.15.	Over trench 93. Infantry call to A/112.	
		9.30.	Trench about C.10.c.5.4. Infantry call to A/112.	
		4.0.	Retaliation.	
		5-30.	Enemy very resentful of damage done to parapet.	
			Observer od D/112 sniped in a tree and from a tree about 150 yards off behind our 101. It is believed that the snipers keep their rifles up in the trees permanently. A/112 moved 1 Gun to alternative position. Details attached.	
	10/10/15.	P.M. 1-15. to a.m.	Covering trenches. 90. to 101. No. of rounds fired. 71/A. About 20 medium H.E. Shell Hostile fire, fired from 90 deg. bearing. Took 15" to arrive at N.A.	
		11-20.	Test retaliation and calls from Infantry.	
		4-30.	D/112 made alternative position for 2 Guns.	
			Observed by D/112 that road running east from PONT ROUGE has been marked by trees.	
		4-10.	C/112 Registration for Wire cutting. Details attached.	

1875 Wt. W593/826 1,000,000 4/15 J.B.C. & A. A.D.S.S./Forms/C. 2118.

Army Form C. 2118

WAR DIARY

or

~~INTELLIGENCE SUMMARY~~

(Erase heading not required.)

Instructions regarding War Diaries and Intelligence Summaries are contained in F. S. Regs., Part II. and the Staff Manual respectively. Title Pages will be prepared in manuscript.

Place	Date	Hour	Summary of Events and Information	Remarks and references to Appendices
LE BEZET	11/10/15		Covering trenches 90 to 101. Hostile fire on O.P. in 93 Trench observation and direction not possible. No. of Rounds fired. 465/A. 10/AX.	
		1.a.m.	G.O.C. 25th Divisional Artillery visited Brigade Headquarters, and ordered the proposed positions for wire cutting to be taken up at once. O.C. pointed out that it meant occupation of exposed positions by daylight, and was given written instructions to carry on. With assistance of G.O.c and his Brigade Major, Waggon lines were roused out and the positions occupied by 2 Guns A/112, and 2 Guns B/112. The latter were clear of the dangerous ground by 5-30.a.m.	
		a.m. 5-30.		
		a.m.	daylight began soon after 4-30.a.m. Fortunetley the enemy were not alert.	
		9-30. to 4 p.m.	Registration for wire cutting by A/112 2 Guns, and C/112. B/112 too exposed, so ordered not to fire. D/112 reports the buildings S. of Chimney C.5.b.5.4. to be important. Messages coming and going. A communication trench is being made to this house.	
		a.m. 8-45	D/112 retaliation and set an enemy observation post on fire.	
		3.55 p.m.	One gunner casualty from A/112 from wire cutting position. Probably a M.b. at long range. Hit in thigh.	
		8-30. p.m.	The telephone communication for Batteries split up are very difficult.	
	12/10/15	10.am. to	Covering trenches 90 to 101. Rounds fired 21/a 3/AX. Hostile fire. Nil. A, B, & D/112 fired a few rounds at request of Infantry.	
		10.15. pm.	Men observed in house mentioned yesterday in blue & white capbands. General staff think probably Cap covers.	
		10.30	Wire is noticed cut by the inhabitants.	

Army Form C.2118

WAR DIARY
or
INTELLIGENCE SUMMARY
(Erase heading not required.)

Instructions regarding War Diaries and Intelligence Summaries are contained in F.S. Regs., Part II and the Staff Manual respectively. Title Pages will be prepared in manuscript.

Place	Date	Hour	Summary of Events and Information	Remarks and references to Appendices
LE BIZET.	13/10/15.	P.M. 3 to 5	Covering trenches 90 to 101. Rounds fired 932/A Hostile fire vigorous on BARKINHAM R.RM and Trenches 90 to 93. This was in retaliation for our action below. Consisted of &7.m.m. & Minewerfer, and 3 H.E. in another direction. O.Ps. became untimable. One 77.m.m. fired H.E. from East of FRELINGHEN.	
		2 to 3-50.	Wire cutting by C/112. 2 Guns A/112. 2 Guns B/112.	
		3.40. to 5.	General engagement by whole Brigade. Communications and reports worked well. O.Ps. Parties much commended for time they remained in exposed O.Ps. viz. Major. NORTON, captains Campbell AURET. B.S.M. of C/112 & B/112 and telephonists. Fire accurate but too diffused for wire.	
		P.M. 6.45.	Sniper fired at Lieut. Col. O.C. Williamson Oswald, near his billet. was quite close	
	14/10/15.	P.M. 3 to 5	Covering Trenches 90 to 101. No of rounds fired 41/A 1/AX. Hostile fire Nil. on guns. rounds 77.m.m. near trenches.	
		4-45.	Retaliation by A/112, C/112, D/112. New structure like large net over stout posts at C.4.d.3.3. reported by C/112 & A/112. A/112 2 Guns & B/112 2 Guns resumed original positions.	
		9.pm.	D/112. Snipers post 8 rounds (opp T.95.)	
	15/10/15.	p.m. 5-30.	Covering trenches 90 to 101. No. of rounds fired. 47/A 4/AX. Hostile fire 20. from 77.m.m. A/112 on German Battery C.5.b.5.4 about.	
		11.a.m.	D/112 Snipers post opp T.95.	
		1.20. to	B. & A/112 at request of infantry.	
		4-30.	Weather misty whole day. No damage to C/112 from fire.	
		6.pm.	A/112 3 rounds on G. Battery to silence them.	
		10-30 p.m.	D/112. S.O.S.	

Army Form C. 2118

WAR DIARY
or
INTELLIGENCE SUMMARY
(Erase heading not required.)

Instructions regarding War Diaries and Intelligence Summaries are contained in F. S. Regs., Part II and the Staff Manual respectively. Title Pages will be prepared in manuscript.

Place	Date	Hour	Summary of Events and Information	Remarks and references to Appendices
LE BIZET.	16/10/15.	p. 1.45. 3-15. 12-30. 9-30.	Covering Trenches 90 to 101. Rounds fired 54/A 32/AX. Hostile fire, about 40. 77.mm shrapnel from S.E. No damage to B/112. Weather very misty. Machine Gun emplacement by C/112. C.10.b.5.9. A/112. 58 rounds at two Houses which harbour Snipers in LE TOUQUET. O.C. 8. N. Lancs. C/112. House said to contain Snipers in LE TOUQUET -do- D/112. 1 Round request of Infantry.	
	17/10/15.	12. noon to 4-30 9.pm. & 11. 6-30. 11.	Covering Trenches 90 to 101. No of rounds fired 59/A. 44/AX. Hostile fire, NIL. B/112 on Machine Gun. D/112 trenches opposite 95 - 96. at Infantry request. C/112. Registration of houses & bridge in FRELINGHEIN. Misty, cleared at night with moonlight. A/112 test on night line. D/112. -do- D/112. -do-	
	18/10/15.	11.am. 1.15. 9.a.m. to 6.30. 11-30. pm.	Covering trenches 90 to 101. Rounds fired. 98/A, 54/AX. Hostile fire. 25 rounds 6" H.E. (?) S.E. from Ploegsteert. Range very long. Report from C/112 of mine under Trench 94. C/112 covers trench 94. A/112. covers to south of line as far as bridge from 94, for night lines. Night lines of B/112 adjusted to cover from D/112, to North Edge of 101. Test A/112. A? B, C, & D/112 at request of Infantry. 10.a.m. C/112 at support entrance to mine. 10-30. B/112 registration of Pontoon Bridge behind White Farm. Caused much retaliation. This is a sore spot as is Bricquetterie. Fire is seldom directed in several directions at once by enemy; it may be due to paucity of guns. Good day for observation. D/112 Support and communication Trenches. from 90 to 101.	

Army Form C. 2118

WAR DIARY
or
INTELLIGENCE SUMMARY
(Erase heading not required.)

Instructions regarding War Diaries and Intelligence Summaries are contained in F. S. Regs., Part II. and the Staff Manual respectively. Title Pages will be prepared in manuscript.

Place	Date	Hour	Summary of Events and Information	Remarks and references to Appendices
LE BIZET.	19/10/15.	P.M. 12.25 to 3-30. 10.a.m. for whole day.	Covering Trenches 90 to 101. Rounds fired. 55/A. 15/AX. Hostile fire bearing from C.7.c.2.8. 87.deg. Time fize at 49. Also houses round LE TOUQUET. probable direction from North of BLANCHISSERIE. C/112. D/112. against points harbouring O.S. & snipers it is supposed. A/112. reports his line to Infantry unsatisfactory as he can't call them up. Weather good for observation. B/112 troubled with air craft. A bridge has been made under the permanent bridge at PONT ROUGE. There is a good deal of traffic over it. Crowds coming and going, and 1 Field Gun was seen. There is a Khaki screen which was blown aside and allowed the observer at LE TOUQUET to see this.	
	20/10/15.	Am. 5-30. to 3-45. p.m. 9-35. to 12.nn.	Covering trenches 90 to 101. Rounds fired 62/A. 14.AX. Hostile fire. Nil. A. & C. fired at request of Infantry. Met G.O.C. R.A. and was shown his wishes as regards localities for 2 Guns in close supports. Weather Misty.	
	21/10/15.	5-30. am. to 4.5.pm. 1.5.am.	Covering trenches 90 to 101. Rounds fired 113/A 27/AX. Hostile fire. Nil. A. B. C. & D. fired at request of Infantry; test and retaliation. C/112. at Maching Gun emplacement. C.4.d.4½.¾. and C.4.d.2½.3. D/112 with H.E. blew up a large sheet of Iron. Batteries report extreme traverse as follows. A/112. North. U.28.d.2.8. South. C.17.d.7.5. B/112. " U.28.a.5.8. " C.10.b.5.5. C/112. " C.4.a.7.8. " C.17.a.0.8. D/112. " U.22.d.2.3. " C.11.b.5.8.	

1875 Wt. W593/826 1,000,000 4/15 J.B.C. & A. A.D.S.S./Forms/C. 2118.

Army Form C. 2118

WAR DIARY
or
INTELLIGENCE SUMMARY
(Erase heading not required.)

Instructions regarding War Diaries and Intelligence Summaries are contained in F.S. Regs., Part II. and the Staff Manual respectively. Title Pages will be prepared in manuscript.

Place	Date	Hour	Summary of Events and Information	Remarks and references to Appendices
LEBIZET.	22. 10. 15.	Noon. to 2-45.	Covering Trenches 90 to 101. Rounds fired, 39/A, 12/AX. A.B. & C/112. Fired at in retaliation at Working Parties. C/112 registered PONT ROUGE. Bridge S.O.S. from A/112. not in working order. Hostile Fire on LE BIZET. Both LE BIZET and B/112 were troubled by Air craft. We did not repel enemy by Air craft guns. These seem somewhat slow to fire. No damage done. Weather clear.	
		6.pm.	A/112 over Trench 91 at request of Infantry.	
	23 10 15.	11-15am. to 3-55.pm.	Covering Trenches 90 to 101. Rounds fired 104A. 32/AX. Hostile fire. 3 rounds. H.E. in square C. no damage. A. B. C. & D/112. Registration and retaliation and fire effect. A/112 at Salient Sand Bag Redoubt. C/112. M.G.E. C.4.d.4½.2. D/112, White Farm, and opposite 100-99. Foggy weather, observation impossible except to about 500 yards from observer.	
	24 10 15	noon to 5.p.m.	Covering Trenches 90 to 101. Rounds fired. 15/A. 23/AX. Hostile fire. Nil. A.B.C. & D/112 Searching and at observation stations (suspected). B/112 at Maching Gun. Weather misty.	
	25. 10. 15.	11.am. 12-34. 2.a.m. to 2.p.m. 9-40.pm.	Covering trenches 90 to 101. Rounds fired. 21/A 17/AX. Hostile fire. Nil. A. & C/112. fired. C. 1 test. A. at Co-operative Chimney for effect. Also at sand bag redoubt. Weather wet. A/112 reports rain is crumpling up revetments. Sand bags giving way. S.O.S. of A/112.	
	26 10 15.	5-45. am. to 4-22.pm.	Covering Trenches 90 to 101. Rounds fired 110/A and 29/AX. Hostile fire. Nil. A. B. C. & D/112, registration. working party. U.24.c.10.0. by C/112. Coop Chimney. C/112. working party at Palace A/112. Registration to N. Flank outside area by B. & D/112. Weather clear. Enemys sausage balloon 70.deg mag from A. 69 deg from C.7.a.3.5.	

Army Form C. 2118

WAR DIARY
or
INTELLIGENCE SUMMARY

(Erase heading not required.)

Instructions regarding War Diaries and Intelligence Summaries are contained in F. S. Regs., Part II. and the Staff Manual respectively. Title Pages will be prepared in manuscript.

Place	Date	Hour	Summary of Events and Information	Remarks and references to Appendices
LE BIZET.	27/10/15.	11.am to 10.pm.	Covering trenches 90 to 101. Rounds fired. 21/A 20/AX. Hostile fire. Nil. B.C. & D/112 registration by B/112. Chimney by B/112 by request of Infantry. 1 Gun run up for direct hits. 3 out of 4 H.E. blind. C/112 Enemy using road E of PONT ROUGE BRIDGE. D/112. Test & SNNXX S.O.S. (4 rounds) Weather wet at times.	
		Noon.	Lieut. Vincent and 20 Picked men went to a review.	
	28/10/15.		Covering Trenches 90 to 101. Rounds fired. 31/A. Hostile Fire. Nil. Weather very wet.	
		10-30.am.	A.C. & D/112. Registration of trenches opposite 102 and 106, by A/112, off C.11.b.5.8. by D/112. Suspected working party at C.4.d.4½.3. by C/112. Communications were worked from borrowed O.Ps. and with borrowed lines for all Batteries as localities were were out of usual zones. A party of men with officers went through a gas lecture and test. 2 Officers were made to feel sick, and 2 men had to be treated for gas poisoning.	
	29/10/15.		Covering trenches 90 to 101. Rounds fired, 74/A and 9/AX. Hostile fire. Nil. Weather better.	
		10-15.am. to	A. B. C. & D/112 retaliation and working parties. D/112 searching road from FRELINGHAM to PONT ROUGE.	
		8.p.m.	New work reported by C/112. at U.24.c.10.0. During the misty weather, new knife rests also made.	
	30/10/15.		Covering Trenches 90 to 101. Rounds fired. 57/A 8/AX. Hostile fire about 8 rounds. at 11.45.a.m. 77.mm. H.E. & B.H.Q.	
		5-40.am. to	A.B.C. & D/112, Registration, retaliation and at working parties.	
		noon.	C/113 at large farm about C.11.d.1.3. The point of the German Salient C.10.b.4.4. LE TOUQUET is being much strengthened. Should be destroyed or may enfilade our trenches with M.G. fire. Special report from Lieut. McKay, A new bridge C.5.c.6.8. and that mariners have been seen.	

Army Form C. 2118

WAR DIARY
or
INTELLIGENCE SUMMARY

(Erase heading not required.)

Instructions regarding War Diaries and Intelligence Summaries are contained in F.S. Regs., Part II. and the Staff Manual respectively. Title Pages will be prepared in manuscript.

Place	Date	Hour	Summary of Events and Information	Remarks and references to Appendices
LE BIZET.	31/10/15.	12. noon. 3.p.m.	Covering Trenches 90 to 101. Rounds fired. 212/A 9/AX. Hostile fire. Nil. A. & C/112. A/112 saw 1 German fall in a working party opp trench 93. C/112 destroyed Factory Chimney C.11.c.7.8. used as O.P. and sniping post. This is a satisfactory action, as the chimney has annoyed us. A/112. F.O.O. Saw 4 sailors in caps with tuft on top in sunken road near BLANCHISSERIE.	

J C Williamson Oswald
LT. COL., R.F.A.
COMMANDING 112th BRIGADE R.F.A.

112th Bde: RFA.
fol 2

121/7708

25th Buorum

Nov 15

Army Form C. 2118

WAR DIARY
or
INTELLIGENCE SUMMARY
(Erase heading not required.)

Instructions regarding War Diaries and Intelligence Summaries are contained in F.S. Regs., Part II. and the Staff Manual respectively. Title Pages will be prepared in manuscript.

Place	Date	Hour	Summary of Events and Information	Remarks and references to Appendices
LE BIZET.	1/11/15.	am. 5-30. to	Covering Trenches 90 to 101. Rounds fired. 35.A. 24 AX. Hostile Fire. Nil.	
		12-45. pm.	A/112. Registration where working parties seen. and for effect on M.G. emplacement N. end of BRASSERIE and on Bridge.	
		3-20. pm.	D/112 Test on German Trench. Weather very wet in afternoon½	
	2/11/15.	a.m.	Covering Trenches 90 to 101. Rounds fired, 41A, 14 A.X. Hostile fire. Nil.	
		9-30. to 7-30. pm.	A & C/112. Sunken Road & Working Parties. 7-30.pm. D/112. Searching for Transport on road PONT ROUGE to FRELINGHEN. Weather raining.	
	3/11/15.		Covering Trenches. 90 to 101. Rounds fired. 38A. AX. Nil. Hostile from 77.mm. Guns. none observed actually.	
		10.am. to 3.pm.	A. C. & D/112. on Working Parties. Trench C.4.d.3.3. by C/112. Houses Near C.5.b.4.4. by D/112. German Trenches probably flooded out, as many men seen in the open and fired on. A fine day and good light. C/112 Battery Headquarters behaved well under shell fire.	
	4.11.15. noon. to 8-30.pm.		Covering Trenches 90 to 101. Rounds fired 61A. 27.AX. Hostile fire. Nil. A. B. & D/112 registration Farm at U.29. d. 30. by A/112. Chimney and Houses C.5.b.58. D/112. open sights. Not much damage to chimney by the hits as yet. B/112 on Road fro. BLANCHISSERIE to FRELINGHAM for Transport by A/112 at 8-30.pm. Transport over Pontoon behind WHITE FARM 6-30 to 8.pm. Battle line reported by A/112 not working to Battalion Headquarters. Weather very wet.	

Army Form C. 2118

WAR DIARY
or
INTELLIGENCE SUMMARY

(Erase heading not required.)

Instructions regarding War Diaries and Intelligence Summaries are contained in F.S. Regs., Part II. and the Staff Manual respectively. Title Pages will be prepared in manuscript.

Place	Date	Hour	Summary of Events and Information	Remarks and references to Appendices
LE BIZET.	5/11/15	12-40.pm.	Covering Trenches 90 to 101. Rounds fired 94A. 4.AX. Hostile Fire on Salient, by 77.mm. H.E. about 30 rounds. Enemy counterstafed in reply to our own Artillery fire for first time in 3 weeks. Sandbag work at U.29.d.50. clearly visible. Appeared to be a gun emplacement to A/112.	
		8.m. 10-15. to 4-20. pm.	A. B. C. & D/112. registration and stop movement.	
		6.pm. to mdt.	D & B/112. Houses bC.5.b.4.3. and Pontoons behind WHITE FARM. to search for Transport. Weather fine. Waggon lines very muddy but getting comfortable. Enemy had sausages up. Several aeroplanes about, Nationality not clear, but those recognised were British.	
		7.pm.	A/112 1 round test.	
	6/11/15.	Pm.	Covering Trenches 90 to 101. Rounds fired 173A. 29AX. Hostile fire. Nil. Weather dry, byt very foggy.	
		8-30. to 4.am.	B. & D/112 on communications and Transport. Battery salvoes at irregular intervals. A/112 reports a green canvas screen erected behind enemys front trench opposite S end of 94 Trench.	
	7/11/15.	11am. to 5-15. pm.	Covering Trenches 94 to 101. Rounds fired. 17Ax. AX. Nil. Hostile fire. Nil. Snipers House by A/112. Well shelled at 11.am. to noon. B. & C. on Working parties Weather very misty.	

Army Form C. 2118

WAR DIARY
or
INTELLIGENCE SUMMARY

(Erase heading not required.)

Instructions regarding War Diaries and Intelligence Summaries are contained in F.S. Regs., Part II. and the Staff Manual respectively. Title Pages will be prepared in manuscript.

Place	Date	Hour	Summary of Events and Information	Remarks and references to Appendices
LE BIZET.		6.am. to 4-30.pm.	Covering Trenches 90 to 101. Rounds fired 68A, 21.AX. Hostile fire Nil. A. B. C. & D/112. Retaliation and for effect. A/112 by their fire yesterday, caused the fall of a house. A/112 on Sunk Road C.5.a.6½.2., and report 4 enemy killed and 4 wounded. C/112 Hit sandbags of suspedted O.P. in first floor window of BLANCHISSERIE Cottage, also the ESTAMINET where small parties seen entering. D/112 over trenches 97 & 98. B/112 Trenches from 101 to 96. in retaliation. Weather very clear. Enemy must have an O.P. near ESSEX Central as fire is fairly accurate to north of it.	

1875 Wt. W593/826 1,000,000 4/15 J.B.C. & A. A.D.S.S./Forms/C. 2118.

Army Form C. 2

WAR DIARY
or
INTELLIGENCE SUMMARY
(Erase heading not required.)

Instructions regarding War Diaries and Intelligence Summaries are contained in F.S. Regs., Part II. and the Staff Manual respectively. Title Pages will be prepared in manuscript.

Place	Date	Hour	Summary of Events and Information	Remarks and references to Appendices
LE BIZET.	9/11/15.	am. 5-30. to 2-15.pm.	Covering Trenches 90 to 100. Rounds fired 133/A. 27/AX. Hostile fire 14 rounds. 77.m.m. LE TOUQUET. A.B.C. & D/112. Searching for Battery E of FRELINGHAM Machine Gun enplacement by B/112 at C.4.a.8.6. Obtained 5 hits by Lt. Moore. Working Parties by C/112 and retaliation and breastwork U.29.b.8.3. Enemy have ceased using sunken road C.5.a.8.2. and crawl to positions by day.	
		2-15	A/112 at Howitzer at U.2.9.b.5.4. in PONT ROUGE moving South.	
		1-30. to 2-30.	Lt Mackay reports movement at Cross Roads U.29.b.27: including Howitzer - also 3 Wagons with white covers, not ambulance and some 80 men including motor cyclists going to and fro. 2 Men at Trench opposite 94 had round grey caps with red cap bands. Neighbourhood of LE BIZET shelled by a Howitzer 16 to 20 rounds. Weather fine Trenches dryer.	
	10/11/15.	am. 9-45 to 10-15 am.	Covering Trenches 94 to 101. Rounds fired 145/A 2/AX. Hostile fire about 20 rounds in C.14 from 77.m.m. bearing 104 to 110 deg Mag. Range over 4000 x Killed 1 horse wounded horse. Registration by A, B, & C/112. Working parties by A/112 hit 2 men 6-30.pm. and C/112 hit 2 men at 9-30.a.m. Houses in C.6.a. and C.5.b.5.4. hit by D/112 known to contain men, also A/112 road near DEULEMONT bridge U.30.b.2.5. Weather wet and squally. C/112 registered houses at V.19.c.9.8. probably. D/112 at working party in hedge C.4.b. disposed. Weather showery.	

Army Form C. 2

WAR DIARY
or
INTELLIGENCE SUMMARY
(Erase heading not required.)

Instructions regarding War Diaries and Intelligence Summaries are contained in F. S. Regs., Part II. and the Staff Manual respectively. Title Pages will be prepared in manuscript.

Place	Date	Hour	Summary of Events and Information	Remarks and references to Appendices
LE BIZET.	11/11/15	10 am. to 3.pm.	Covering Trenches 90 to,101 Rounds fired 105/A. 5/AX. Hostile fire from 77.m.m. 30 rounds H.E. from about C.11.c.9.4. 16 to 20 rounds on C.14.d. from E. of FRELINGHIEN. 10 rounds from C.5.c.8.5. to enfilade trenches to N. 6 H.E. near PLOEGSTEERT: from near PONT ROUGE or WHITE FARM.	
		10-15 am. to 8.pm.	A. B. C. & D/112 Registration on working parties behind water tower by A/112. Billets in C.5.b.5.4. by D/112 and to intercept transport C.5.b.10.6. at 8.pm. and trenches C.5.b.4.9. enemy ~~constantly~~ dispensed. completly	
		2.pm. to 6.pm.	Waggon Lines are wiring where ever possible A/112 at BRASSERIE. Much shouting heard.	
	12/11/15.	am.	Covering trenches 90 to 101. Rounds fired 105 A. 11.A.X.Hostile fire from C.6.b. 4 rounds. Howitzer.	
		10-30 to 6-30 pm.	A. & D/112. House behind Brasserie. registration. Machine Guns opposite 100 trench. M.G. stopped by D/112 and traffic U.30.c. and located flash in rear of barn in U.30.c. Weather showery but very clear between showers. Enemy's lines showing up as the leaf falls.	
		10.pm.	Enemy shelled ARMENTIERES and PLOEGSTEERT. No damage reported.	

Army Form C. 2

WAR DIARY
or
INTELLIGENCE SUMMARY

(Erase heading not required.)

Instructions regarding War Diaries and Intelligence Summaries are contained in F. S. Regs., Part II. and the Staff Manual respectively. Title Pages will be prepared in manuscript.

Place	Date	Hour	Summary of Events and Information	Remarks and references to Appendices
LE BIZET.	13.11.15.	10.20. am.	Covering trenches 90 to 101. Rounds fired. 6/A. Hostile fire none to report. A/112 Dug out N. of BRASSERIE. Great storm and rain. A yellow flag with black cross spread out open in trench South of BRASSERIE reported by A/112.	
	14.11.15.	Pm. 1-30. to 2.5. p.m.	Covering Trenches 90 to 101. Rounds fired 21/A, 3 AX. Hostile fire. None to report. A/112 on Vats at BLANCHISSERIE for suspected snipers and M.G. Weather good.	
	15.11.15.	a.m. 10-30. to 3-45. pm.	Covering Trenches 90 to 101. Rounds fired 129/A. 8/AX. Hostile fire reported. 15.C.M. Howitzer. 6 rounds. Covering 74th Infantry Brigade as from 30.9.15. Weather hazy. A. B. C. & D/112 mainly for registration)A/112. C.18.d.5½.5½)B/112. C.18.d.9.6. O.P. Chimney. U.30. A.B.C. & D/112 in order to be ready to support an attack)C/112. C.11.b.4.9.)D/112. C.12.a.5.1. (a Battery not located). by 21st Division to South. Dispersing Working Parties V.19.c. by C/112.	
	16.11.15.	Am. 10-30. 10.0. to 3-50. pm.	Covering trenches 90 to 101. Rounds fired 185/A. 5/AX. Hostile fire about, 50 77.mm. on Barkenham, Lukers & Trench 93. A.B.C. & D/112 fired to distract enemy from affirs to North by Canadians, 7th Infantry Brigade and 110th Brigade, R.F.A., fired on various targets. Enemy erecting a wire entanglement in front of support trench at C.4.d.7.1. to 3. Weather misty except from 2-45.p.m. to 3-15.p.m.	

Army Form C. 2

WAR DIARY
or
INTELLIGENCE SUMMARY
(Erase heading not required.)

Instructions regarding War Diaries and Intelligence Summaries are contained in F.S. Regs., Part II. and the Staff Manual respectively. Title Pages will be prepared in manuscript.

Place	Date	Hour	Summary of Events and Information	Remarks and references to Appendices
LE BIZET.	17.11.15	P.M.	Covering Trenches 90 to 101. Rounds fired. 56/A. 2AX. Hostile fire.	
		12-40.	15 C.M. about 15 rounds in B.12. bearing 115° Mag. Angle of decent 45° from B.12.	
		2-30.	-do- 5 Rounds. C.7.	
		2-30.	10.5.c.m. 5 rounds B.12. bearing 91.Mag. Angle of descent 61°.	
		3.15. to 3.	Also 50 to 60 rounds 77.mm. on LE TOUQUET probably near C.18.a. & b. German Balloon and Aeroplane near WARNETON took advantage of a short lull in storm to register ranges. Our plane and baloons stopped this when they went up. A pity it was not done earlier.	
		3-20.		
		10.am.	A battle practice drill was given by G.O.C. 25th Divisional Artillery. in which all battery objectives were given by him. All Lt. Cols. had to do was to detail the battery. The O.Ps. did not work well as only one stall covered the ground and this was taken up by an Officer, B/113 R.F.A., who only allowed 10 minutes to B & D/112 for observation. The exercise created many problems which require clearing up. Shell fire cut wires. Weather frosty turning to rain about 9-30.pm.	
	18.11.15.		Covering Trenches 90 to 101. Rounds fired 486/A.	
		12.	Cold & frost in morning. Afternoon rain.	
		noon	Hostile fire 6 H.E. Roads & Buildings C.7.d. Also LE BIZET. Flashes observed by D/112 in line C.5.d.8.5. - C.6.c.2.5.	
		10.am	A/112 C.18.d.5½.5. B/112 O.P. in U.30.d. & FRELINGHEIN PONTOON.	
		12.55.	C. FmcLENARD. D/112 Battery at C.12.a.5.1. These were in retaliation for the shelling of ARMENTIERES - which in turn was shelled owing to this distribution of FT.SENARMONT. J.19. by 3rd H.A.R. supported by 21st Divisional Artillery.	
		pm.		
		10.pm.	D/112 various targets during night in retaliation. Weather slightly haze. Enemy's Aeroplanes active.	
	19.11.15.		Covering Trenches 90 to 101. Rounds fired. 44/A Hostile fire. Nil.	
		am.	Weather misty.	
		10-45. to 3.pm.	A/112 & D/112 various points for Corking Parties in the fog., & Trenches opposite 95 to 97.	
		8.pm.& night.	Various points in zone.	

Army Form C. 2

WAR DIARY
or
INTELLIGENCE SUMMARY
(Erase heading not required.)

Instructions regarding War Diaries and Intelligence Summaries are contained in F.S. Regs., Part II. and the Staff Manual respectively. Title Pages will be prepared in manuscript.

Place	Date	Hour	Summary of Events and Information	Remarks and references to Appendices
LE BIZET.	20 II 15	Pm. 1-30. to 3.	Covering Trenches 90 to 101. Rounds fired. 78/A.6/AX. Hostile fire on LE TOUQUET road about 30 -77.mm. Shrapnel from D/3.a.8.6. A German flag in LE TOUQUET SALIENT.	
		Am. 10-45. to 2-50.	A.B.C.& D/112 registration & retaliation. B. registered U.21.b.8.2. Weather somewhat hazy. Sharp frost in morning, then thaw.	
	21 II 15	8-33.am. to 3-40.pm.	Covering Trenches 90 to 101. Rounds fired 27/A 5/AX. Hostile fire, none to report. A. & C. A/112 Battery S. of Palace FRELINGHEIN. C/112 on O.P. at U.30.a.2.0½. Possible O.P. of Battery firing on 96. Also in C.4.d.5.1. at working party. A 60 pr Shrapnel case fell in C.14.a.4½.7. Cause not known. Weather cold. Also frost in th emorning.	

1875 Wt. W593/826 1,000,000 4/15 J.B.C. & A. A.D.S.S./Forms/C. 2/18.

Army Form C. 2118

WAR DIARY
or
INTELLIGENCE SUMMARY

(Erase heading not required.)

Instructions regarding War Diaries and Intelligence Summaries are contained in F. S. Regs., Part II. and the Staff Manual respectively. Title Pages will be prepared in manuscript.

Place	Date	Hour	Summary of Events and Information	Remarks and references to Appendices
LE BIZET.	22/11/15	a.m. 11-35. to 3-40.	Covering Trenches 90 to 101. Rounds fired 282/A. 1/AX. Hostile Fire. Nil. Hard frost most of day. Misty with periods of thicker fog. A.B. & C/112 registration & retaliation for bombing of 92 Trench. D/112 Wire cutting. 200 rounds on C.4.d.2.5. 20 yards of supports destroyed. Wire thin and could not be seen.	
	23/11/15.	a.m. 9.57. 8-50.	In support of trenches 94° to 101. Rounds fired A.57 AX. 6. Hostile fire, nothing to report A/112 School House on C.T. here. D/112. Retaliations opposite T.96. Weather fine. some frost and fog.	
	24/11/15.	2-45. to 4-30 10.a.m. to 3.55.	In support of Trenches 94 to 101. Rounds fired 118.A. 21.A.X. Hostile Fire 24 rounds from FRELINGHIEN on LE TOUQUET. K.K.MM. 16 rounds 10.5.cent½ from U.29.d. or U.30.c. 20 rounds tt.mm. LE TOUQUET C.5.a. or b. A.B. & C/L12 retaliation and registration. C/112 hit one man at V.19.c.2.6. B. & C. special retaliation for ARMENTIERES and DEULEMONT. Good day for observations. Frost all day.	
	25/11/15.	Covering 94° to 101. 11-15. 10.am.	Rounds fired. 92.A. AX. 23. Hostile fire 4 rounds light How. 77.mm. 60 to 80 rounds LE TOUQUET from E. of FRELINGHIEN and on road from MOTOR CAR CORNER from LA HOUETTE. GERMAN MACHINE GUN HOUSE very tender spot. Weather, Clear morning and misty afternoon. A. B. C. & D/112 Hostile Parties German Machine Gun House - Retaliation and registration. B. C. & D/112 Battle practice a few rounds	

Army Form C. 2118

WAR DIARY
or
INTELLIGENCE SUMMARY

(Erase heading not required.)

Instructions regarding War Diaries and Intelligence Summaries are contained in F. S. Regs., Part II. and the Staff Manual respectively. Title Pages will be prepared in manuscript.

Place	Date	Hour	Summary of Events and Information	Remarks and references to Appendices
LE BIZET.	26. II 15.	am. 10-45.	Covering Trenches 9¾ to 101. Rounds fired. 119/A 45/AX. Hostile fire. 12. H.E. 77.mm. on LE TOUQUET. Range about 4000 yards. E. of FRELINGHIEN. Also 50 to 60. 77.m.m. on LE TOUQUET from C.18..d. or D.13.a.	
		10.am to 2-40.pm.	A, B, C, & D/112 Retaliation and on Working Parties C.5.b.5.9. 2 Howitzers spotted from C.5.b.9.3. Enemy made a dead set on LE TOUQUET & 12 H.E. in LE BIZET. about from C.13.a.9.9. 870° M.N.	
	27. II 15.	am. 11. to	Covering Trenches 9¾ to 101. Rounds fired.108.A. 25.AX. Hostile fire. None to report. A. B. & C/112 Retaliation C.4.d.1.7. & C.4.d.2.5½	
		2-45. and pm. 3-50.	C.6.b.5.0. Parties on road U.24.d.6.9. V.19.c.1.0. - V.19.c.9.9. Hostile battery is near C.6.b.5.0. also U.30.c. A large burst of flame and smoke at C.4.d.3.3. - perhaps for a gas attack. Weather fine with frost.	
	28. II 15.	8.am. to 1.pm.	Covering Trenches 9¾ to 101. Rounds fired 104.A. 15.AX. 30 to 40 77.mm. from LA HOULETTE on LE TOUQUET to LE BIZET road at parties of troops. Observed fire.	
		12.noon. to 3.pm	A.B.C. & D/112. Ratateliation and registration. Hostile section at C.5.b.9.3. at request of 13th Cheshires. Dug out U.30.c.0.8.	
			Cottage at C.8.d. used as a ranging point by 7.7.mm LA HOULETTE. O.P. in Trees near VACHERIE FME or in FRELINGHIEN.	
		3-50	Thick smoke as yesterday.	
		4-55.pm.	Flash of gun apparrently at C.11.b.8.7.. 90° Mag from BARKENHAM.	

1875 Wt. W 593/826 1,000,000 4/15 F R.C. & A. A.D.S.S /Forms/C. 2118.

Army Form C. 2118

WAR DIARY
or
INTELLIGENCE SUMMARY
(Erase heading not required.)

Instructions regarding War Diaries and Intelligence Summaries are contained in F.S. Regs., Part II. and the Staff Manual respectively. Title Pages will be prepared in manuscript.

Place	Date	Hour	Summary of Events and Information	Remarks and references to Appendices
LE BIZET.	29 11 15.	2.pm. to 3.10 pm. 8-15.am.	Covering Trenches 94 to 101. Rounds fired A.218 AX. 92. Weather wet, no frost, very stormy towards night. Light fair for observation. Hostile fire 6 to 8 rounds by 10.5.cm. on LE BIZET: also 16 H.E. on same from Hows. probably at U.30.c. or d.- 4.77 mm. rounds on LE TOUQUET×road. whole mile probably smothered by prompt retaliation on LA HOULETTE and O.P. as below. A. B. C. & D/112 took on a connected attack at prominent points suspected of O.Ps. viz:- FRELINGHIEN: at C.11.c.7.1. at Chimney & Billets near U.30.d.2.4. At battery at C.5.b.9.3. reduced from 30' to 50' innocuous, at Chimney & billets near U.30.c.6.6. which was	
	30 11 15.	9.am. to 2.pm. 8.pm.	Covering trenches 94 to 101. Rounds fired 83/A.9/AX. Weather mild and fine High wind. Hostile fire from 77.mm. at LA HOULETTE. D.13.a.2.1. about 60 rounds on points between LE TOUQUET & MOTOR CAR CORNER. This looks like observed fire owing to insufficient screening of communication trenches and roads and to opening up of country by winter conditions. 77.mm. N.E. of BLANCHISSERIE also fired on LE TOUQUET about 15 rounds. 10.5. C.M. from E. of FRELINGHIEN fired 6 rounds on LE TOUQUEN at noon. A. B. C. & D/112 on Working Parties at DEULEMONT U.30.b., V.19.c. to V.25.a. Suspected O.Ps at BARRACKS, chimney at U.30. house C.11.c.8.1. were kept under occasional fire. Heavy Battery was assisted by our observations to get on battery at D.13.a.2.1. To sum up the month, the enemy batteries have more to shoot at, but are being kept under as we have more to shoot at under winter conditions.	

M. Williamson Oswald
LT. COL, R.F.A.
COMMANDING 112th BRIGADE R.F.A.

112th Madr. R.Fs.
Vol: 3

121/7909

25/6/72

Army Form C. 2118

WAR DIARY
or
INTELLIGENCE SUMMARY

(Erase heading not required.)

Instructions regarding War Diaries and Intelligence Summaries are contained in F.S. Regs., Part II. and the Staff Manual respectively. Title Pages will be prepared in manuscript.

Place	Date	Hour	Summary of Events and Information	Remarks and references to Appendices
LE BIZET.	1/12 15.	10-30 am. & 3.pm.	Covering Trenches 90 to 101. Rounds fired. 38.A. Nil.AX. Hostile Fire. LA HOULETTE D.13.a.2.1. About 20 rounds 77.mm. on MOTOR CAR CORNER, and 4 rounds Square. C.14. This Battery now appeared to be kept under by our arrangement with C/95, R.F.A. on our right to take it on, and to our watch on its possible O.Ps at FRELINGHIEN.	
		9.am. to 2-15.pm.	A.B.C. & D/112 on Working Parties and parties of troops, V.19.c. & C.30.b. Occasional rounds at suspected O.Ps in churches at WARNETON & DEULEMONT and at O.P Chimney in U.30. also Guns. Light very good in morning - misty in afternoon. 3 or 4 Waggons and occasional small parties of men were seen moving along roads E of DEULEMONT.	
2/12 15.		2-10. pm.	Covering Trenches 90 to 101. Rounds fired. 26.A. Nil.AX. Hostile fire 4 rounds 7.7.cm. D.13. on LE TOUQUET from LA HOULETTE. D. Some rounds from 10.5.cm. U.30. towards OOSTOVE FARM about 1.pm. D.13.a.2.1.	
		10.am. to 12-45.pm.	Only 2 Batteries were available for C.R.A. Battle Practice, Viz:- B. & D. A. B. & D/112 Battery N. of PONT ROUGE, not located by A/112 as too far out of Zone. U.30.d.1.4. Barracks.	
		7.pm.	Communication Trenches opp. 96. & 99 by D & B/112. Ricochet 105 C.M. picked up with an uncommon fuze. Weather fine, fairly clear.	
		7.pm.	Hostile mine near 99. blown up. Held by 9th L.N. Lancs.	
3/12 15.		5.a.m. to 101.	Covering Trenches 90 to 101. Rounds fired 19.A. 5 AX. Hostile Fire nothing to report. Very wet in afternoon. Misty and damp in morning. Batteries stood by in case enemy rushed trench 99, also later for a 9.22 shoot at LE TOUQUET A/112 1 round.	
4/12 15.		7.a.m. 11-50 to 5.pm.	Covering Trenches 94 to 101. Rounds fired 44.A. 1.AX. 12 Rounds H.E. near A. & C.7. Hostile fire from 10.5.c.m. believed behind LES OURSINS FME or LE FALOT. 7.7.mm. 6 rounds from LA HOULETTE. Hostile fire after dark allowed flashes to be seen.	
		2.pm. to 6-35 pm.	A. B. C. & D/112 on CROWN PRINCE FARM, on C.17.a.1.8. C.29.b. traffic in V.19.c. BLANCHISSERIE & DURIEZ FARM, Mostly retaliation. Variable with good light after noon. Weather misty rainy in the morning. One set flashes locate gun at C.18.d.8.6. This is one of the LA HOULETTE GROUP.	

1875 Wt. W593/826 1,000,000 4/15 J.B.C. & A. A.D.S.S./Forms/C.2118.

Army Form C. 2118

Instructions regarding War Diaries and Intelligence Summaries are contained in F.S. Regs, Part II. and the Staff Manual respectively. Title Pages will be prepared in manuscript.

WAR DIARY
or
INTELLIGENCE SUMMARY
(Erase heading not required.)

Place	Date	Hour	Summary of Events and Information	Remarks and references to Appendices
LE BIZET.	5/12. 15.	am. 7-30. to 3-30.	Covering Trenches 90 to 101. Rounds fired 10.A. Nil.AX. Hostile Fire Nil. A. B. & C/112. C.5.d. FRELINGHIEN. DEULEMONT Bridge in road all at working or exposed parties Weather Foggy. Hazy.	
	6/12. 15.	12-30. to 1-30.	Covering Trenches 90 to 101. Rounds fired. 102.A. 31.AX. Hostile Fire:- worried by .7.7.cm. shrapnel & H.E. about 20 rounds in C.14. from LA HOULETTE D.13.a.2.1. or C.18.d.8.6.	
		8-30. to 3-30.pm.	A. B. C. & D/112. on LES ECLUSES to & PONT ROUGE Road - M.G. at C.10.b.5.9. U.30.b.1½.3. - V.19.c. C.6.d.7.8. One man for certainty so probably more. All above for effects on exposed parties. O.Ps and registered points fired on at request of O.C. 11. Lancs. Fusiliers.	
		11-30. am.	C/112 firing at LES ECLUSES was taken by War Office Bioscope. Light very good indeed. Chimney S.W. of DEULEMONT has a square hole in it facing South, perhaps an O.P.	
		3.pm.	8 Men put in an ambulance at D.1.b. believed wounded from dugout C.6.d.7.8. destroyed by C/112.	
	7/12. 15.	8-30.am. to 9-15. am.	Covering Trenches 90 to 101. Rounds fired. 98.AX. Nil.AX. Hostile Fire about 46.7.7.mm. shrapnel & H.E. from E. of Frelinghien on PLOEGSTEERT road and Trenches. About 20.7.7mm. on C.8.c. from LA HOULETTE D.13. About 30 7.7.mm. from BLANCHISSERIE direction on C.8. Hostile O.Ps looking on C.8. are DEULEMONT CHURCH, Bic Chimney N of BLANCHISSERIE, Chimney near DEULEMONT CHURCH.	
		9.am. to 4-45. pm.	A. B. C. & D/112 Retaliation on FRELINGHIEN BRIDGE & BARRACKS? & BLANCHISSERIE WOOD. Working Parties at U.29.d.5.0. PONT ROUGE & LES ECLUSES Road. LE TOUQUET to FRELINGHIEN Road - at C.6.d.7.8. to D.1.c.1.5. Water overflowed from U.29.b.0.9. to U.29.d.9.7. about, and the Trolly way at C.5.a.3.2 only just above water. Also visible in front of BLANCHISSERIE. Light good in morning, hazy in afternoon.	
	8/12. 15.	9-15. am. to 2pm.	Covering Trenches 90 to 101. Rounds fired 110.A. 15.AX. Weather very clear all day. Hostile fire 2 rounds 7.7.mm. from N.E. - 6 from LA HOULETTE. - 6 rounds 13 or 15.cm. from 7° R. of DEULEMONT CHURCH. 15. H.E. on O.P. 16.	
		7-30am to 3-45am.	A.B.C. & D/112. on working parties C.11.a.2.0. - C.4.b. trolly line. FRELINGHIEN - V.19.c.3.6. Road S.E. of PONT ROUGE BRIDGE.19.c.9.8. - V.26.d.2.2. - U.30.b.4.6.	

Army Form C. 2118

WAR DIARY
or
INTELLIGENCE SUMMARY
(Erase heading not required.)

Instructions regarding War Diaries and Intelligence Summaries are contained in F.S. Regs., Part II. and the Staff Manual respectively. Title Pages will be prepared in manuscript.

Place	Date	Hour	Summary of Events and Information	Remarks and references to Appendices
LE BIZET.	8/12 15. Contd.	7.30. am 3-45.am.	The enemy have only 2 apparent lines of communication from East of the LYS RIVER to LE TOUQUET. FRELINGHIEN Road and Trolly Line from C.4.b. to C.5.a. Men seen using Plank Bridge at C.5.a.4.1. Not generally used by day.	
	9/12 15.	7.a.m. to 4-45.pm.	Covering Trenches 90 to 101. Rounds fired 25.A. 4 AX. Hostile Fire. NIL. Weather misty. No view. A/112. on Parties FRELINGHIEN. also PONT ROUGE Retaliation. D/112. Battery behind BLANCHISSERIE WOOD. To Silence.	
	10/12 15.	3.pm. to ½ 4-15.pm. 11.am. to 4-10.p.m. 7.pm. to 4.45.pm.	Covering Trenches 90 to 101. Rounds fired 151.A. 26 AX. Hostile Fire 24.77.MM. Behind 95 Trench from E. of FRELINGHIEN 8. H.E. on O.P. 15. which is getting much attention. Weather misty in morning, light improved in afternoon. A/112. Cutting communications of LE TOUQUET & on M.G. N. of LE TOUQUET. D/112 BLANCHISSERIE WOOD & U.30.c.0.9. & O.P. A/112. to catch working party on LE TOUQUET to FRELINGHIEN ROAD. Batteries located by flashes at D.2.00.d,5.5. about and L.2.b.9.2. about.	
	11/12 15.	11-30. am. 11-30. am. 10.15. am.	Covering Trenches 90 to 101. Rounds fired. 46.A. 5 AX. German Lines at LE TOUQUET cut off except from Sq. C.4.b. & rafts at C.5.c.7.7. & c.11.c.5.7. with precarious road, C.11.c.4½.8½ to POND HOUSE. Hostile Fire on C.14 - 20 rounds, 10.5.cm. from N.E. of BLANCHISSERIE WOOD. Weather clear. Weather clear. A. B. C. & D/112 rafts - parties on PONT ROUGE to LES ECLUSES Road. Houses at V.19.c.9.9. Road S.E. of PONT ROUGE Bridge when parties are seen to double for about 80 yards Long Plank Bridge C.5.a. totally submerged.	
	12/12 15.	12.pm.	Covering Trenches 90 to 101. Rounds Fired 42.A. 13.AX. Hostile Fire. NIL. River LYS risen another two feet. Raft of barrels now used to fill in FRELINGHIEN to LE QUOUQUET ROAD - U.29.c.7.1½. is a vulnerable point, only communication from PONT ROUGE to SOUTH. A. B. C. & D/112. on Barrells in FRELINGHIEN C.6.a.1½.8.	

1875 Wt. W593/826 1,000,000 4/15 J.B.C. & A. A.D.S.S./Forms/C. 2118.

Army Form C. 2118

WAR DIARY
or
INTELLIGENCE SUMMARY
(Erase heading not required.)

Instructions regarding War Diaries and Intelligence Summaries are contained in F. S. Regs., Part II. and the Staff Manual respectively. Title Pages will be prepared in manuscript.

Place	Date	Hour	Summary of Events and Information	Remarks and references to Appendices
LE BIZET.	12/12 15. Contd.	12-35.pm.	Battery in C.12.a. or C.6.c. Flashes seen behind BLANCHISSERIE WOOD. Hostile Battery ceased firing exact time. QUESNOY CHURCH & O.P.16. Weather clear.	
	13/12 15.		Covering Trenches 90 to 101. Rounds fired. 464A. 74AX.	
		12.15. to 2-30. pm.	About 12.77. & 10.5.cm. on LE TOUQUET from N.E. of BLANCHISSERIE WOOD. A combined shoot with 25 H.A. Battery 9.2" - Canadian 60 prs, - 111th & 113th Brigade, R.F.A. to bolt Germans from Salient which is practically an Island with CROWN PRINCE FARM half submerged. Enemy kept very still but must have lost. Batteries which retaliated confined to SILENT SUSAN at C.12.a. or b. Field Howitzers and perhaps a 7.7. f.m. Battery in rear of BLANCHISSERIE WOOD and the LA HOULETTE BATTERY. May have moved to shell ARMENTIERES.	
		twx212 noon.	Battery at C.5.b.8.2½ silenced.	
	14/12 15.	2-40.pm.	Covering Trenches 90 to 101. Rounds fired 120.A. 19.AX. Hostile Fire NIL. Weather Hazy.	
		9.am. to 3-45. pm.	A German aeroplane passed from Houplines over LE BIZET. Not fired at by our A.A. Guns A. B. C. & D/112. mounds at C.4.d.3.0. Parties at U.30.c.4.3. - C.5.b. trench - O.P. C.5.b.6.9. Road S.E. of PONT ROUGE BRIDGE.	
	15/12 15.	12-3pm	Covering Trenches 90 to 101. Rounds fired 92.A 34.AX. Hostile Fire. NIL. Ambulance and parties seen in C.6.d. going East. Weather clear.	
		10-5. am.	Chimney stated to be in U.30.d.9.5. believed to be in V.25.a.3.7. Columns of water and materials thrown up at C.4.b.5.5. when B/112 fired at it. No retaliation which is unusual and seems to open with paucity of Guns reported on 13th instant.	
		9-30.am.	A. B. C. & D/112 on U.30.d. - C.6.d. Roads S.E. of Pond House Bridge and Pont Rouge Bridge	
		3-30pm to	La Haire, Battery in rear of BLANCHISSERIE. Weather fine, somewhat hazy.	

Army Form C. 2118

WAR DIARY
or
INTELLIGENCE SUMMARY

(Erase heading not required.)

Instructions regarding War Diaries and Intelligence Summaries are contained in F.S. Regs., Part II. and the Staff Manual respectively. Title Pages will be prepared in manuscript.

Place	Date	Hour	Summary of Events and Information	Remarks and references to Appendices
LE BIZET	16/12/15.	8-30. am. to noon.	Covering Trenches 90 to 101. Rounds fired. 63/A 61.AX. Hostile fire NIL. Weather misty. A. B. C. &D/112. on FRELINGHIEN. U.29.b.8.2. working parties. C.4.d.3.4. a mound. ~~Extrkrt.~~ C.4.b.5.5. working party.	
	17/12/15.	10.am. to noon.	Covering Trenches 90 to 10. Rounds fired 44.A. 2.AX. Hostile fire. NIL. River LYS fallen again about 2 feet. Battle Practice took a few rounds.	
		10-45.am to 3.17.pm.	A. B. & D/112. M.G. at BRASSERIE - C.4.b.5.5. PONT ROUGE Road & Bridge, working parties. Cut FRELINGHIEN Road to LE TOUQUET.	
		6-10.pm.	D/112 opposite T.95 at request of 11th Lancs Fusiliers. Weather thick & in morning very dark in spite of moon.	
	18/12/15.		Covering Trenches 90 to 101. Rounds fired 47.A 11.AX½ Hostile fire NIL. River LYS has fallen. Trolly line near BRIQUETERIE in full view again. Weather foggy - moon bright at night.	
		11.am. to 3-15.pm.	A. B. C. &D/112. Wooden Bridge N.W. of BLANCHISSERIE WOOD. C.4.b.5.5.& past & parties. Experimental firing by C.R.A. General Bethell of 25th Divisional Artillery, 3 rounds from a Gun platform approached by a windlass up a ramp, proposed for close support.	
	19/12/15.	9.am. to 10.am.	Covering Trenches 90 to 101. Rounds fired 75. A. 19.AX. Hostile fire 10. rounds 15.cm. Gun. H.E. from East of Blanchisserie on Le Bizet. Battery N. of LE QUESNOY near Railway. East Water in LYS much lower. Enemy active sniping all night. Road D.l.b. used by 4 horsemen/and a trap West. Weather clear and good for observation.	
		10.25. am.	A. B. C. & D/112. at C.17.a.4.3. for retaliation for mine - to break causeway.	
		9.am.	Letouquet to Frelinghien - Pont Rouge Road 3 men hit, possible more. Working party at C.4.b.5.5.	
		3-30. pm.	Parties at road S.E. of Pont Rouge Bridge at C.6.d.8.6. at V.19.c. Cross Roads.	
		8-15. pm.	D/112. Retaliation at request of Infantry. 11th Lancs Fusiliers. T.98.	

1875 Wt. W593/826 1,000,000 4/15 J.B.C. & A. A.D.S.S./Forms/C.2118.

Army Form C.2118

WAR DIARY
or
INTELLIGENCE SUMMARY
(Erase heading not required.)

Instructions regarding War Diaries and Intelligence Summaries are contained in F.S. Regs., Part II. and the Staff Manual respectively. Title Pages will be prepared in manuscript.

Place	Date	Hour	Summary of Events and Information	Remarks and references to Appendices
LE BIZET.	20/12. 15.	3-15. pm.	Covering Trenches 90 to 101. Rounds fired. 29.A. Nil. A.X. Covering Trenches Hostile fire from probably LA HOULETTE 77.mm. 6 rounds at C.8. Weather very misty.	
		11-15. am. to 3.pm.	A. & D/112. Le Touquet to Frelinghien Road and probable battery at C.12.a.	
	21/12. 15.	7-30. noon.	D/112 over T. 95. in retaliation.	
			Covering Trenches 90 to 101. Rounds fired. N.A. 49 AX. Hostile Fire NIL. Very misty - observation on Front Trenches only. D/112 Mounds. at C.4.d.3.3. A successful venture - rendered it useless. 33% hits & H.E. detonation good.	
	22/12	12-15 pm.	Covering Trenches 90 to 101. Rounds fired. 38.A. 48.AX. Hostile Fire 3 rounds in Sq. C.10. Crater 20 ft in diameter. 5 ft deep. a 21.cm mortar probably bearing located from DEULEMONT Man in Steel Helmet going S.E. at U.30.b. Le Touquet to Frelinghien Road rebuilt. Weather became misty.	
		9. am.		
		10. am.		
		9-15.am.	A. B. C. & D/112 to silence M.G. C.17.a.3.6. roadway at C.11.a.3.0. over Trench 98 Infantry call 9th L. N. Lancs. Trench opposite T.96. This is strongly wired for 30 yards - enemy put over some 60 77.mm. in return which were ill directed. Their observation always appears to be from near their Gun positions and these appeared unobserved in the mist.	
	23/12 15.	11-30. am.	Covering Trenches 90 to 101. Rounds fired 64.A. 50.AX. Hostile fire 10.5. cm. and 1 21.cm. round in C.7. from Deulemont. Same mortar as reported 22nd Dec. 1915.	
		12-15.	There are always Troops at La Tache, parties of 25 men moving N. dispersed and road stopped till 3.p.m. when it got dark. 125 men in all passed.	
		10-25. am. 9-30.am. to 3.pm.	Men mending wire near U.30.b.2.7. 9 men and one horse bagged for certain. by C/112. A. & C/112. at Pont Rouge. Iron Bridge U.30.b.2.4. Working Party, working party. Troops at DOLLS HOUSE & U.24.d.1.1. at U.30.b. at V.2.6.d. Weather clear.	

Army Form C. 2118

WAR DIARY
or
INTELLIGENCE SUMMARY
(Erase heading not required.)

Instructions regarding War Diaries and Intelligence Summaries are contained in F. S. Regs., Part II. and the Staff Manual respectively. Title Pages will be prepared in manuscript.

Place	Date	Hour	Summary of Events and Information	Remarks and references to Appendices
LE BIZET.	24/12/15.	2.45.pm.	Covering Trenches 90 to 101 Rounds fired 124.A. 38.AX. Hostile Fire. NIL. Weather dull but clear. Traffic at V.26.d.3.3. La Tache about 8 to 10 vehicles an hour mostly going South.	
		3-30.pm.	7 men bagged in all at various points by A/112 & C/112.	
		&	A. B. C/112 on road C.11.a.3.0. Pont Rouge C.11.b.3.9. C.4.b.6.5. V.19.c. & d.	
		10-28	V.26.d.3.2. - Raft at C.5.c.6.8.	
	25/12 to	3-28.		
	25/12/15.		Covering Trenches 90 to 101. Rounds fired. Nil. A. Nil.AX. Hostile fire 2 Rounds 77.cm. from LA HOULETTE D.13. Weather clear in morning, afternoon misty. (some showers) A good deal of aeroplane work occurred.	
	26/12/15.	9-30.am.	Covering Trenches 90 to 101. Rounds fired 277.A. 58.AX. 10 rounds 77.cm. from Blanchisserie wood silenced at 10.am. by C/112.	
		am.	7 H.E. 10.5.pm. Deulemont.	
		10-50 to 3.pm.	B. C. & D/112 respectively cut wire for. prearranged minor operations at C.4.a.7.4. C.10.b.5.9. and C.4.d.½.7. the latter being the real entrance point. A. B. C. & D/112. at Pont Rouge Road at traffic. Water tower where machine gun reported.	
		10.am.	trench over 94. O.P. C.5.b.9.1. Battery in Blanchisserie wood which was stopped by C/112. Chimney at U.30.d.2.3. Weather hazy, clear at intervals. Water in LYS risen 2 feet. Gap in Frelinghien - Letouquet Road widened. Observers plainly seen at Chimney U.30.c.7½ & at Deulemont. Water at U.24.d.0.1. up to Dolls House. No troops using the breastwork. Pont Rouge Bridge damaged and traffic ceased.	
	27/12/15.	9.am.	Covering Trenches 90 to 101. Rounds fired. 58.A. 54.AX. Weather hazy 15.cm. in morning, clear at intervals during afternoon. Hostile fire 15.c.m. 30 H.E. 13.cm. at V.19.c.9.9. about 40 rounds. 8 rounds 77.mm. from D.13. 10.5.cm. 30 H.E. 20 H.E. 10.5. place unknown.	
		11-15.am.	D/112 continues wire cutting at C.4.d.½.7. & M.G. at C.4.d.3.4. which was silenced.	
		11.am.	A. & B/112. Barracks. C.11.c.8.1. suspected O.P. Water Tower C.11.c.5.3.	
		to 1-30.pm.	O.P. Chimney. U.30.d.2.3. Deulemont Church.	

Army Form C. 2118

WAR DIARY
or
INTELLIGENCE SUMMARY
(Erase heading not required.)

Instructions regarding War Diaries and Intelligence Summaries are contained in F.S. Regs., Part II. and the Staff Manual respectively. Title Pages will be prepared in manuscript.

Place	Date	Hour	Summary of Events and Information	Remarks and references to Appendices
LE BIZET.	28/12 15.	am 10-35. to 12.45.	Covering Trenches 90 to 101. Rounds fired 963.A. 88.AX. A. C. & D/112 at Pont Rouge Road. Chimney U.30.d.2.3. 77. Battery behind BLANCHISSERIE WOOD. Minor Operation & Hostile Fire is distributed in attached report. Weather clear all day. This was unfortunate as it gave away our forward guns firing on German Fire Trenches and which had to be withdrawn at night.	
	29/12 15.	10.am. to 12.30.pm.	Covering Trenches 90 to 102. Rounds fired 39.A. Nil.AX. Hostile fire NIL. Weather hazy all day. Rain in evening. D/112. first experience of aeroplane observation on Battery at C.12.a.5.1.	
	30/12 15.	10-30. to 1pm.	Covering Trenches 90 to 102. Rounds fired 58.A. 16.AX. A.&C. on LE TOUQUET SALIENT, Chicken Run & BRASSERIE. C.10.b.5.3. - C.17.a.3.4. - C.17.a.6.3. and raft at C.11.a.6.5. 89 & 88 Trenches were being bombarded by heavy guns & minewerfer.	
	31/12 15.	am. to 2-30. pm.	Covering Trenches 90 to 102. Rounds fired 129.A. 38.AX. Hostile fire by 4 Batteries. Deulemont 10.5.cm. V.20.a. 15.cm. BLANCHISSERIE WOOD 77.mm. LA HOULETTE. D.le. 77.mm. LES OURSINS. C.24.a.-Central- about 100 to th 150 rounds at C.9. where old gun positions were bombarded. Also 6 rounds from D.13. at C.14. drawn by Infantry of 2nd R.I.R.	
		7-15. to 11-15.pm.	A. C. & D/112. on Pont Rougé Road & Screen Salient LE TOUQUET - FRELINGHIEN - working party DEULEMONT Bridge Chimney U.30.d.3.2. V.19.c. at Traffic. Houses near FME DURIEZ. Battery behind BLANCHISSERIE WOOD. D/113 at request of 9th L.N. Lancs over trenches 95 & 97. Weather fine & clear.	

J. Williamson Oswald
Lt. Col. R.F.A.
Commanding, 112th Brigade, R.F.A.

A.S/301.   SECRET.

Report of 112th Brigade, R.F.A. Night of 28.12.15., - 29.12.15.

Sheet 1.

Operation of Night 28th - 29th December, 1915.

The following previous orders were issued yesterday:-

I am covering the attack at 2 points namely, C.4.a.9.0. about C.4.d.½.7. by the Lancashire Fusiliers and an attack on LE TOUQUET SALIENT by the Cheshires. The Cheshire attack is timed by the Fusiliers attack.

The Fusiliers attack is covered by 3 Batteries. B. Battery on night lines U.29.c.0.2., C.4.b.9.7., C.4.b.7.5. with one gun at C.21.a.1½.9½., firing straight down the railway at C.4.b.4.4.

D. Battery on night lines from C.4.d.5.6. to C.4.b.2.2.

C. Battery on night lines from C.10.b.8.7. to TWIN COTTAGES.

These Batteries are observing their fire so as to shorten range with safety to our own Infantry

A. Battery has one Gun at LYS FARM to fire on parapet at C.10.b.6.2. or neighbourhood if required, by O.C. Cheshires, and 2 guns to fire on C.10.b.5.6. with one gun to fire on M.G. near WATER TOWER, FRELINGHIEN. Signal for the attack will be given by Colonel Crosbie, guns will fire continuously in B. C. & D. Batteries for 30 minutes.

In "A" Battery for 5 minutes, then a cessation, and then for 4 minutes. 75 Rounds a gun allowed for the above. A. Battery is in touch with O.C. Cheshires, the remaining Batteries are in touch with Colonel Crosbie, who has Lieut Letts with him to communicate orders to me. Should I require further assistance I shall ring up 111th Brigade for 50 rounds from a Battery on the NECKLACE, and 95th Brigade to fire on FRELINGHIEN 50 rounds.

OC Williamson Oswald
LT. COL., R.F.A.
COMMANDING 112th BRIGADE R.F.A.

Sheet 2.

The previous orders were carried out at 9-45.p.m.

It will be seen that the Batteries of the 112th Brigade, R.F.A. had to stand a certain amount of Shell Fire. I have no reports from the two Batteries of other Brigades, nor from the 60 pr. Battery Canadians, who also assisted efficiently. I beg to bring forward the names of Captains, Campbell, Auret, Barker, and Lieut Vincent. Lieut MacKay efficiently observed at the salient at LE TOUQUET, and was knocked over by a minewerfer.

In the previous operation of wire cutting and battering down the enemy parapet at C.4.d.½.7. Map 36. D/112 R.F.A. were most efficient and cut a hole through the wire and parapet. 2 Guns under Lieut Radcligfe went forward to a position at a range of 1,400 and battered the parapet and cut the wire on point C.4.d.½.7., for 3 days in succession, 26th 27th, 28th.
The observation was carried out at about 36 yards distance by periscope by Captain Barker, assisted with Lieut. Ive, with B.S.M. T.E. Bateman. This Warrant Officer was so close to the firing that one shell slightly off line, bulged the exterior of the parapet he was observing over. He was also knocked over by a minewerfer exploding near him.

These two guns were ultimately found by the enemy on the 28th instant and suffered somewhat in material.

The details are as usual embodied in the Daily Report compiled from those of the Batteries.

The telephones worked up in efficiency during the last 3 months, and by 2nd Lieut. D.L. Carr, Orderly Officer, worked very well and talk was plain.

I beg to forward the above names of Officers and also the following W.O. and Rank & File.

No. 22338. B.S.M. T.E. Bateman, of D/112.
No. 53912. Sergeant E.G. Gregory)   )
No. 24472. Sergeant T.W. Fitzgerald.) Nos 1. of Wire cutting Guns.
No. 63307. Bombardier T. Gray.   )
No. 60601. Gunner E. Barham.   )   Telephonists.

De Williamson Oswald
Lt. Col. R.F.A.
Commanding, 112th Brigade, R.F.A.

A.S/301.   S E C R E T ?

Supplementary Report of the Minor Operation of the night
28th - 29th December 1915
_____

  The following information is added to my original report.

  The arrangements as verbally issued were carried out with the following exceptions.

  The guns opened at 9-40.p.m. 28th December 1915, at 9-43.pm. "Stop" came through, and on enquiry from Lieut Letts, I was informed it was a correct order. Almost immediately the order to fire was again given and the guns opened at 9-46.p.m.

  I understand that the hole cut in the parapet and the wire at C.4.d.½.7. during the 3 previous days by D/112 R.F.A., was sufficient for the/Infantry to enter the front trench and was 7 to 101 yards wide. This appears an entirely satisfactory opening.

  A/112 R.F.A. opened fire on the WATER TOWER, FRELINGHIEN, and on C. Trench near German Machine Gun House at 10.p.m. through a misunderstanding.

  The communications were by voice through the telephone from 2nd Lieut Letts. at ESSEX CENTRAL FARM to O.C. D/112, R.F.A., and from him to the Batteries and to me at Headquarters.
This method was adopted as owing to the faintness of the line it was not safe to plug me through to Lieut Letts: To save seconds I ordered Captain Barker, O.C. D/112, R.F.A. to transmit orders to open fire direct to the Batteries of the 112th Brigade.
He did this and fire was duly opened by B. C. & D. A queried the order and ultimately consented to fire at 10.pm. I do not attach importance to this mistake as C/112 R.F.A. was firing close to German Machine Gun House and A/95, R.F.A. close to the WATER TOWER FRELINGHIEN on the scheme for the 111th Brigade, R. Lanc. Fusiliers so that any alarm likely to be caused by "A" was discounted.

The objectives were as follows:-

112. 2 Guns ranges 3400 dropping to 3300 on German Machine Gun House.
   1 Gun, range 3800 on WATER TOWER - FRELINGHIEN.
   No. F.O.O. owing to opening fire prematurely.

- 2 -

Guns, range 4100 dropping to 3600 on line from C.4.b.1½.10. to C.4.b.1½.7.

1 Gun firing from C,21.a.1½.9½., range 3000 to 2500 (searching enfilade fire along railway) on line from C.4.b.7.10. to C.4.b.3.0. Observing Officer at O.P. (Observation Farm).

C/112. 4 Guns ranges 2500 dropping to 2400 on German Second Line Trench and after about 20 rounds to 2350.

Observing Officer at O.P. (Estaminet - LE TOUQUET) also constant telephonic communication with Infantry in 94 Trench.

D/112. 2 Guns ranges 3500 dropping to 3450 for No.4. Gun, and 3450, dropping to 3350 for No.1. Gun on C.4.b.4.1.

2 Guns, ranges 3500 dropping to 3450 for No.3.Gun and 3450 dropping to 3350 for No.2. Gun, on C.4.d.3.4.

F.O.O. in Trench 95.

B/111. THE NECKLACE.

D/95. FRELINGHIEN.

The Batteries shelléd were as follows:-

A/112. Very heavy whiz - bang retaliation at 10.10.pm. No observation possible.

B/112. Wire cutting section shelled during the day by 15 rounds H.E. 15.c.m. Field Gun, and 10.5.cm. Howitzer at 1pm., and 30 rounds H.E. 10.5.cm. Howitzer from 2-30 to 3-30.pm.

Owing to the time taken for our Infantry in the Hostile Trenches to return to our own trenches, Artillery Fire was continued till 10-37.pm.

B/112. ~~B/112.~~ 12 rounds at 10.p.m. Magnectic bearing of scoops 105°.

At about 11-30.pm. I had arranged as follows:-

Captain Campbell to use A/112 and C/112 R.F.A. for the scheme at LE TOUQUET SALIENT and was allotted 600 rounds 18.pr for it.

I allotted 300 rounds to A/112 R.F.A., 250 to C/112. R.F.A. and retained 50 rounds in hand.

I spoke over the telephone to Captain Campbell and put him in charge under Major Reeves 13th Cheshires. I told Captain Campbell if he wanted more help to let me know. It was difficult to speak and also to give very explicit orders without giving too much away should there be Hostile Listeners tapping the line.

but I gathered it was satisfactory.

I also asked A/95 R.F.A. to be prepared for a call and that they might have 50 rounds for it, same objective.

I also warned B. & D/112, R.F.A. that there was an off chance they might be wanted, but otherwise to resume ordinary.

At 1-10.a.m. Captain Campbell opened fire and fired a few rounds in support when the operation ceased.

30th December, 1915.
                                            Lt. Col. R.F.A.
Commanding, 112th Brigade, R.F.A.

25th. DIVISIONAL ARTILLERY

112th. BRIGADE R. F. A.

25th. DIVISIONAL ARTILLERY

JANUARY 1 9 1 6.

112. RFA
25.º Dez.
Vol. 4

Army Form C. 2118

WAR DIARY or INTELLIGENCE SUMMARY

(Erase heading not required.)

112/Bde. R.F.A.
JAN 1916.

Place	Date	Hour	Summary of Events and Information	Remarks and references to Appendices
LE BIZET.	1.1.1916.	10.am.	Covering Trenches 90 to 102. Rounds fired. 48. A. 10. A.X. Hostile Fire. Nil. Weather very windy with squalls from S.W. At night a gale. A. B. C. & D/112 on Pont Rouge Road - over 102. Trench. - U.30.c.0.8. at Working Party - near White Farm, C.4.b.	
		to 2.15.pm.		
	2.1.16.		Covering Trenches 90 to 102. Rounds fired. 51. A. Nil. A.X. Hostile fire. NIL. 3 New loop holes in house at C.11.b.6.3. Weather generally misty and rainy.	
		11.am.	A. B. & D/112. at Support Trenches LE TOUQUET - at PONT ROUGE Road at Troops.- LE TOUQUET to FRELINGHIEN road to destroy. O.P. Chimney. U.30.d.2.3. - Sniper in C.4.b.	
		8-40.pm.	D/112 a Salvo at Snipers trees in C.4.b.	
	3.1.16.		Covering Trenches 90 to 102. Rounds fired 145.A. 60.A. Weather clear and light good. Hostile fire from 15.cm. from DEULE MONT about 35 rounds at C.7. 10.5.cm. from DEULE MONT. & LES ECLUSES on C.7. & 14. about 50 rounds. 30 H.E. 15 & 13.cm. on LE BIZET from near DEULEMONT.	
		10.30.am.	A. B. C. & D/112 at Working Parties C.17.a.2.8. - C.11.c.2.9. at wooden bridge - 6.11.a.5.2. DEULEMONT CHURCH a certain O.P.; O.P. at U.30.d.2.3. DURIEZ FARM and Farm, C.5.b.5½.9. LA TACHE V.26.d.2.3. - C.4.d.½.7½ M.G. & stray point. Traffic U.30.c. to C.6.b. Batteries in rear of BLANCHISSERIE	
	4.1.16.		Covering Trenches. 90 to 102. Rounds fired 59.A. 1. AX. Hostile fire. NIL.	
		7-15.am.	A. B. C. & D/112 at PONT ROUGE Road an early movement. Church at FRELINGHIEN used as a Cook House. O.P. in House U.30.c.1.9. - O.P. at U.29.d.5.½. - O.P. Chimney at U.30.d.2½.2.	
		12.45.pm.	Over Trench 95. Weather very dull. Fine rain in afternoon.	
	5.1.16.		Covering Trenches 90 to 102. Rounds fired. 86. A. 21. A.X. Hostile fire NIL.	
		12x50 RM.	A. B. C. & D/112. working parties at C.10.b.9.8. - at C.5.b.9.1. - Houses V.19.c.9.9. - to C.5.b.5.4. Weather clear. A trolly way appears to have been made on Road South of PONT ROUGE Bridge.	
		5x15PM		46
	6.1.16.		Covering Trenches 90 to 102. Rounds fired. 60A. 25.AX. Hostile Fire 28 rounds H.E. from 15 or 13.cm, on C.10.a.	
		12.50.	Retaliation from 15.c.m. at DEULEMONT stopped when Church was fired at. A.B. & C/112 over Trench 94 - at Houses C.17.a.9.6. and C.17.b.3.10. - On LE TOUQUET SALIENT DEULEMONT CHURCH O.P. Farm at C.5.b.5.9.	

Army Form C. 2118

WAR DIARY
or
INTELLIGENCE SUMMARY
(Erase heading not required.)

Instructions regarding War Diaries and Intelligence Summaries are contained in F. S. Regs., Part II. and the Staff Manual respectively. Title Pages will be prepared in manuscript.

Place	Date	Hour	Summary of Events and Information	Remarks and references to Appendices
LE BIZET.	7.1.16.	7.a.m. to 1.pm.	Covering Trenches 90 to 102. Rounds fired 24. A. 3 A.X. Hostile Fire. Nil. A. & C/112. on Deulemont House at C.11.b.4.9½. & U.30.c.1.9. On Pont Rouge to DEULEMONT Road firing on parties. C.11.b.4.9½. is a Dump or O.P.	
	8.1.16.	10.am. to 3.pm.	Covering Trenches 90 to 102. Rpunds fired. 66 A. 30 A.X. Histile Fire. NIL. A. B. C. & D/112. at O.P. in House C.11.b.4.9½. and knocked down. BLANCHISSERIE WOOD at request of Infantry. Parties on PONT ROUGE Road DEULEMONT Road. Suspected O.Ps at V.19. and DEULEMONT CHIMNEY. - O.P. at U.30.d.2.3. LES ECLUSES CHIMNEY. Weather-Clear.	
	9.1.16.	10.am. to 3-30.pm	Covering Trenches. 90 to 102. Rounds fired 81 A. 25 AX. Hostile Fire 100 rounds 10.5.c.m. into C.7. - 13 rounds 10.5.c.m. fro. U. 30. b. 2. 2. into C.14. A. B. C. & D/112 at Houses C.11.b.2.5. and C.11.b.2.6.. suspected as billet. 6 hits. Buildings C.6.a. Parties near DOLLS HOUSE U.24.d.0.1. - Billet V.19. Battery behind BLANCHISSERIE WOOD C.5.d.10.8. Battery in U.30.d. (registered by D/112). The enemy's tactics on imagining they have discovered a Battery appeares to be to fire 110 H.E. shell at this point. This beds too much waste of ammunition on their part.	
	10.1.16.	3-40.2pm. 10-35) to 3.25.pm.)	Covering Trenches 90 to 102.. Rounds fired 34 A. 16 AX. Hostile fire :- 2 Rounds 10.5.c.m. into LE BIZET apparently from direction of D.13. Yesterday's 10.5.c.m. located. A. & B/112. on LE TOUQUET & FRELINGHIEN ROAD which has been greatly strengthened with barrels.	
	11.1.16.	12-20. to 3-30. 8.am.	Covering Trenches 90 to 102. Rounds fired. 63 A 28 A.X. Hostile fire :- 102 rounds 10.5.c.m. & 15.c.m. H.E. into C.14. One round was effective killing one and wounding 3. men of C/112. Movement was seen in O.Ps in DEULEMONT CHIMNEY and Engine House U.30.a.1½.½. A. B. C. & D/112 Various points as on previous days. Fresh point dug out C.5.c.8.2.	
	12.1.16.	10-40.am. to 3.p.m.	Covering Trenches 90 to 102. Rounds. fired 38 A. A.X. Hostile Fire. NIL. D/112 registration on LE TOUQUET Salient for Wire Cutting. C/112 registration for new positions.	

Army Form C. 2118

WAR DIARY
or
INTELLIGENCE SUMMARY
(Erase heading not required.)

Instructions regarding War Diaries and Intelligence Summaries are contained in F.S. Regs, Part II. and the Staff Manual respectively. Title Pages will be prepared in manuscript.

Place	Date	Hour	Summary of Events and Information	Remarks and references to Appendices
LE BIZET.	13.1.16.	9-45.a.m.	Covering Trenches 90 to 102 - Rounds fired 5 A. 18 A.X. Hostile fire. NIL. A. & B/112. U.29.d.5.0. working party - Frelinghien & Le Touquet Road. This road seems very important and is now very strong and should be dealt with by Howitzer or heavy Gun fire to cut it. A/112 has cut it 5 times.	
	14.1.16.		Covering Trench 90 to 102. Rounds fired. 13 A. 4 A.X.	
		9-40.am. to 1-45.pm	Hostile fire about 70 rounds 10.5.cm. at C.4. and LE TOUQUET from LES ECLUSES. C/112 at Dug-outs at foot of Sniper's Poplar - BLANCHISSERIE WOOD to stop bombardment over Trench 94.	
		11-20 to 3.pm.	Air observation for C/112 at C.6.c.8.0. In the LE TOUQUET Salient have been put on uprights apparently to support revetments.	
	15.1.16.		Covering Trenches 90 to 102. Rounds fired. A./10 A.X. 17	
		11-45 am.	Hostile fire on 94 Trench from LES ORSINS - LA HOULETTE and C.12.c.2½.2½. 250 rounds 7.7.mm. 15 rounds 10.5.c.m. from LES ECLUSES Also on B.6. 15 c.m. fired.	
		9-30.pm.	30 .7.7.mm. on LE TOUQUET. 7 rounds at 8000 yards. U.30.a. fired 2 rounds 10.5.c.m.	
		8.am.	A. B. C. & D/112 at usual targets mainly at request of Infantry for above hostile fire, at C.4.b. Sunk Road.	
	16.2.16.	10.40. to 3-45.	Covering Trenches 90 to 102. Rounds fired. 12 A. 14 A.X. Hostile fire Nil. A/112 on FRELINGHIEN LE TOUQUET ROAD, C.4.d. Working Parties on Troily Line.	
	17.1.16.	8-2559	Covering Trenches 90 to 102. rounds fired. 48 A. - A.X. Hostile fire:- rounds 7.7.mm. into LE TOUQUET at 8.p.m. 6 rounds from C.5.d.9½.5½. A. & C/112. CROWN PRINCE FARM - USINE - BRIDGE FRELINGHIEN. Air observation for C/112	
		11-20.am.	at C.12.a.6.4.	
	18.1.16.	10-35 am. to 11 am.	Covering Trenches 90 to 102. Rounds fired. 66 A. 6 A.X. Hostile Fire on LE TOUQUET 90 rounds 7.7.mm. from D.12.c.c.2½.2½. and C.5.d.9½.5½. 15 rounds 10.5.c.m. and 15.c.m from V.30. A. B. C. & D/112. mainly registration C.4.d. Water Tower; C.11.c.4½.0. U.30.d.2.3.; C.10.b.9.3. C.10.b.4.3½. Enemy jumpy last 5 days near LE TOUQUET ARB on it.	

1875 Wt. W593/826 1,000,000 4/15 J.B.C. & A. A.D.S.S./Forms/C. 2118.

Army Form C. 2118

WAR DIARY
or
INTELLIGENCE SUMMARY
(Erase heading not required.)

Instructions regarding War Diaries and Intelligence Summaries are contained in F.S. Regs., Part II. and the Staff Manual respectively. Title Pages will be prepared in manuscript.

Place	Date	Hour	Summary of Events and Information	Remarks and references to Appendices
LE BIZET.	19.1.16.	12.30 pm. to 6-30 pm.	Covering Trenches 90 to 102. Rounds fire. 546. A. 413 A.X. Hostile Fire. Le Touquet received 7.7.mm. - 10.5.c.m. & 15.c.m. fire from all known Batteries, also two 21.c.m. from either Messines, or I.23. or I.29 direction. This caused a good deal of damage. Minor operation completly successful. - reports attached.	
		12-30. to 2-30.	Also Wire Cutting Section D/112 received 15.c.m. & 10.5.c.m. estimated at 50 rounds no less here.	
		2-30.	At Motor Car Corner, 1 man C/112 Mortally Wounded.	
		2.40. to 3-35.	A/112 Frelinghien Church, Brasserie, 28 rounds. one Gun 40 rounds, at 520 yards range breeching Le Touquet Salient 40 rounds. Very good.	
			C/112. Barrage 207 rounds.	
			B/112. Bombardment and barrage 144 rounds & Counter Battery.	
			D/112. Counter Battery. 8 rounds.	
		12.30. to 2-30.	D/112. 310 rounds wire cutting. Very effective. Reports attached. Corps and 2nd Army much pleased.	
	20.1.16.		Covering Trenches 90 to 102. Rounds fired. 27 A. 14 A.X. Hostile Fire NIL. Weather clear.	
		10.am. to 4.	A, & C/112. on Working Parties Le Touquet Salient. Battery at C.12.a.5.1.	
			C/112 Air Observation on Farm C.12.a.6.4. direct hit.	
		6-15. pm.	Armoured cable reported as hit several times last night by splinters and once by "Blind" shell. but was now cut or seriously damaged.	
	21.1.16.		Covering Trenches 90 to 102. Rounds fired. 19 A. 16 A.X.	
		9-55 am. to 4.	Hostile Fire 32 rounds 77.mm. on C.7. from C.11.c. fuzes set at 50 only one in air. A/112 reports Lieut Mackay says absolute quiet in enemy salient. One man 2nd R.I.R. has been right through Salient and found no one there. Enemy are building their first line behind CROWN PRINCE FARM.	
		9-30. am.	A/112 on FRELINGHIEN & LETOUQUET ROAD and on working parties at enemy's Salient LE TOUQUET. B. & D/112. at O.P. U.30.d.2.3. Halte C.11.b, cross at C.11.b. Head of C.T. at C.4.b.4.5. Battery behind Blanchisserie Wood. A/112 now again through to 93 trench.	
	22.1.16.		Covering Trenches 90 to 102. Rounds fired. 47 A. 18 A.X. Weather Showery.	
		9-15. pm.	Hostile Fire 20 rounds 15.c.m. on Ploegsteert.	

1875 Wt. W593/826 1,000,000 4/15 J.B.C. & A. A.D.S.S./Forms/C. 2118.

Army Form C. 2118

WAR DIARY
or
INTELLIGENCE SUMMARY

(Erase heading not required.)

Instructions regarding War Diaries and Intelligence Summaries are contained in F.S. Regs., Part II. and the Staff Manual respectively. Title Pages will be prepared in manuscript.

Place	Date	Hour	Summary of Events and Information	Remarks and references to Appendices
LE BIZET.	22.1.16.		(Continued).	
		9-35.a.m. to 3-20.	A/112 on CROWN PRINCE FARM at Working Parties as opportunity offered. B. & C/112. at White Farm & Billets U.29.d.8.8. Traffic & Buildings at LA TACHE V.26.d.	
	23.1.16.		Covering Trenches 90 to 102. Rounds fired. 118 A. 9 A.X.	
		4-30.pm.	Hostile fire 6 rounds 15.c.m. from Fme Du Chastel on C.7. 3 Blind.	
		9.am	A/112 at Working Parties LE TOUQUET Salient also on FRELINGHIEN.	
		to B/112.	At C.11.b.1.7. Deulemont U,30.d.½.2.	
		4.pm.	C/112. LA TACHE V.26. where many signs of occupation - and PONT ROUGE. Weather clear after a misty morning.	
	24.1.16.		Covering Trenches 90 to 102. Rounds fired. 30 A. 32 A.X. Hostile fire NIL.	
		12-30. to 1-30. pm.	A/112. on working parties in LE TOUQUET and on Water Tower. Le Touquet. B.C. & D/112 on 10.5. Battery at DEULEMONT. 15.c.m. at Los A Moelle - Battery in rear of Blanchisserie wood as 21st Division on our right was carrying out an operation. Weather misty.	
	25.1.16.		Covering Trenches 90 to 102. Rounds fired. 37 A.148 A.X. Weather misty. Relief commenced. 2 Guns each Battery relieved. by 51st Brigade, R.F.A. of 9th Division. Batteries on relief marched to Wagon Lines.	
	26.1.16.		Covering Trenches 90 to 102. Relief completed. Batteries on relief marched to Wagon Lines.	
CAESTRE AREA	27.1.16.		Brigade Marched into CAESTRE AREA into 2nd Corps Reserve for rest and instruction in open tactics.	

J.C.......
LT.COL. R.F.A.
COMMANDING 112th BRIGADE R.F.A.

25th. DIVISIONAL ARTILLERY

112th. BRIGADE R. F. A.

25th. DIVISIONAL ARTILLERY

M A R C H 1 9 1 6.

Army Form C. 2118

112 RFA
Vols 4.5.6.7.

WAR DIARY
or
INTELLIGENCE SUMMARY
(Erase heading not required.)

Instructions regarding War Diaries and Intelligence Summaries are contained in F. S. Regs., Part II. and the Staff Manual respectively. Title Pages will be prepared in manuscript.

Place	Date	Hour	Summary of Events and Information	Remarks and references to Appendices
La Breardes.	February 1916.		No. war Diary was written for the month of February 1916 by Lieut. Col. O.C. Williamson Oswald who relinquished command of the Brigade on the 28.2.16. on being transferred to the 19th Brigade R.G.A. During this month the Brigade was in the REST AREA near CAESTRE, spending 10 days at the WATTEN TRAINING AREA.	
"	March 1st 1916.		Lieut. Colonel B.A. Butler assumed command of the Brigade, vice Lieut. Col. O.C. Williamson Oswald.	
"	March 2nd to 9th.		General Duties were carried out by the Brigade during this period in the REST AREA.	
"	March 10th		Brigade left HAZEBROUCK and marched to BERGUETTE where it remained in billets for the night	
Berguette.	March 11th		Brigade left BERGUETTE at 9.a.m. on the 11th and marched to FIEFS remaining there the night in billets to await further orders from the Division.	
"	March 12th		Orders received that the Brigade was to continue the march to AVERDOINGT. Left FIEFS at 11.a.m. arrived at AVERDOINGT about 4.p.m. on the 12th.	
AVERDOINGT.	March 13th to 17th		Daily Routine by the Brigade and General Training at AVERDOINGT.	
"	17th March		The Colonel Commanding Brigade accompanied by Battery Commander visited Battery positions and Trenches in the area of MONT ST. ELOI and CARENCHY.	
"	March 18th		"A" and "B" Batteries were detailed to go into action with the 46th Divisional Artillery and proceeded from Averdoingt to wagon line area at CAMBLAIN L' ABBE.	

1875. Wt. W593/826 1,000,000 4/15 T.R.C. & A. A.D.S.S./Forms/C. 2118.

Army Form C. 2118

WAR DIARY
or
INTELLIGENCE SUMMARY

(Erase heading not required.)

Instructions regarding War Diaries and Intelligence Summaries are contained in F.S. Regs., Part II and the Staff Manual respectively. Title Pages will be prepared in manuscript.

Place	Date	Hour	Summary of Events and Information	Remarks and references to Appendices
AVERDOINGT.	March 19th		Colonel Commanding Brigade again visited Battery positions and Trenches in the area of MONT St. ELOI. and CARENCHY.	
"	March 20th		"C" and "D" Batteries move from AVERDOINGT to go into action with the 51st Divisional Artillery. Batteries going into action a few days later.	
"	March 21st to 31st.		Brigade Headquarters and Brigade Ammunition Column remained in billets at AVERDOINGT General Duties were carried out during this period.	

Lieut. Col. R.F.A.
Commanding 112th Brigade R.F.A.

25th. DIVISIONAL ARTILLERY

112th. BRIGADE R. F. A.

25th. DIVISIONAL. ARTILLERY

A P R I L 1 9 1 6.

Army Form C. 2118

WAR DIARY
or
INTELLIGENCE SUMMARY
(Erase heading not required.)

1/2 ᵗʰ BDE. R.F.A.
APRIL 1916

Instructions regarding War Diaries and Intelligence Summaries are contained in F.S. Regs., Part II. and the Staff Manual respectively. Title Pages will be prepared in manuscript.

Place	Date	Hour	Summary of Events and Information	Remarks and references to Appendices
AVERDOINGT	April 1st to 3rd.		Brigade Headquarters and Brigade Ammunition Column still in billets at AVERDOINGT. General Duties being carried out.	
NEUVILLE AU CORNET.	April 4th.		Brigade Headquarters and Brigade Ammunition Column move from AVERDOINGT to NEUVILLE AU CORNET leaving AVERDOINGT at 2.p.m. and arriving at NEUVILLE AU CORNET about 4.p.m.	
"	April 5th & 6th		General Duties by the Brigade Headquarters and Brigade Ammunition Column.	
MONT ST ELOI.	April 7th		Brigade Headquarters move to MONT ST ELOI and billet in the old MONASTRY where it remained in billet until the 25th April 1916. During this period the Colonel Commanding reconnoitred the surrounding country and studied the line which the Brigade were about to take over.	
VILLERS AU BOIS.	April 25th		Brigade Headquarters moved into huts in VILLERS AU BOIS and the Brigade Ammunition Column moved from NEUVILLE AU CORNET to billets in CAMBLIGNEUL. ½ Batteries were relieved.	
"	April 26th		Colonel took over Command of Q.Sector, Batteries of the Brigade having relieved Batteries of the 46th Divisional Artillery (with the exception of "B" Battery which did not leave its present position). The remaing ½ Batteries were relieved.	
"	April 27th.		Brigade Headquarters moved from VILLERS AU BOIS to dug-outs in the trenches near CABARET ROUGE.	
	April 25th		The relief was complete by 11.30.p.m. After Dark 25th, fire of all 4 Batteries was concentrated round a supposed mine crater reported to have been blown up opposite the end of CENTRAL AVENUE.	

Army Form C. 2118

WAR DIARY
or
INTELLIGENCE SUMMARY

(Erase heading not required.)

Instructions regarding War Diaries and Intelligence Summaries are contained in F.S. Regs, Part II. and the Staff Manual respectively. Title Pages will be prepared in manuscript.

Place	Date	Hour	Summary of Events and Information	Remarks and references to Appendices
In the Field VILLERS AU BOIS.	April 25th.		After daybreak 26th, The Brigade fired behind 2 supposed mine craters and in response to an S.O.S. Signal. The left hand mine was supposed to be about S.15.c.9½.7½. As the light got better the right hand mine was located as near as S.15.d.1½.1½. The positions of "C" and "D" Batteries were shelled heavily by a 3 gun Battery of about 12 or 15 c.m. from N. or N.E. of GIVENCHY and by field guns about 800 true bearing by sound only from S.23.c.6.3. (No flashes visible") The Brigade fired 1700 rounds.	
"	April 26th		Batteries closely registered the enemy's Front line and Support line trenches also an enemy's suspected Headquarters. 1000 A. and 383 A.X. were fired by the Brigade.	
"	April 27th		Batteries again registered the enem's Front line and support trenches. 269 A. and 84 A.X. were fired by the Brigade.	
In the Field.	April 28th	10.50. a.m. to 11.15. a.m.	"A" Battery fired at Front and Support lines at S.15.c.3.2½. - S.22.a.½.4½. This was asked for by the Infantry. "B" Battery retaliated on S.15.d.central.	
"		1.p.m. to 2.p.m.	"A" Battery again fired on Front line and Support on request of the Infantry. This Battery also fired at the same target at 1.40.p.m. and 2.p.m. at the same request.	
"		12.30. to1.pm.	"B" Battery fired at S.15.d.central in retaliation.	
"		7.40. to 9.30.p.m.	"C" Battery retaliated on S.15.c.7.9. to S.15.d.2.7. "A" Battery fired at S.22.a.0.8. - S.22.a.½.4½. (Barrage on 4.86.) "C" Battery fired at S.15.c.7.9. - S.15.d.2.7. (S.O.S. & Barrage)	
"		1130.a.m.	Hostile fire for this day was as follows:- "A" Battery were shelled by a 7.7.mm. (Suspected position by sound S.23.a.4½.3.	

Army Form C. 2118

WAR DIARY
or
INTELLIGENCE SUMMARY
(Erase heading not required.)

Instructions regarding War Diaries and Intelligence Summaries are contained in F. S. Regs., Part II. and the Staff Manual respectively. Title Pages will be prepared in manuscript.

Place	Date	Hour	Summary of Events and Information	Remarks and references to Appendices
In the Field.			HOSTILE FIRE continued.	
	April 28th	9.45 p.m.	This 7.7.mm. Battery fired 32 rounds at the screen behind "A" Battery, but did no damage. "C" Battery's Reserve position also received some attention the enemy firing about 100 rounds from the direction of LA FOLIE WOOD. This was supposed to be a 10 c.m. Gun, but it did no damage. An Aeroplane was brought down in the direction of VIMY, unable to say whether hostile or mot. Our Batteries fired 1455 A. 299.A.X.	
-do-	April 29th	11.30 a.m. to 9.15pm.	"A" Battery retaliated on the enemy's front line also registered S.22.a.2½.6. - S.22.a.2½.5. This Battery also fired on Communication Trench leading to S.22.a.2½.6. S.15.d.3.2½. - S.22.a.4.4½. were also fired on in response to an S.O.S. Signal.	
"		6.15pm. to 11.30.pm.	"B" Battery fired under instructions from HULL BRIGADE on the following points:- S.21.b.8.3½. - S.15.d.9.3½. - S.15.d.10.2. - S.16.c.1.1. - S.22.a.2.7½.	
"		3.45.pm. to 8.p.m.	"C" Battery Fired at S.15.d.1.9¼. - S.15.d.4.7. in Retaliation for Trench Mortars and also at S.15.d.5½.6. - S.15.d.7.4. (Barrage C. by order of the Brigade Commander).	
"		3.22.pm. to 6.p.m.	"D" Battery fired in retaliation on trenches opposite Q.91.	
"		7.45pm. to 2.a.m.	"D" Battery barraged trenches opposite Q.86 and Hill 145.	
"		6.30 to 8.p.m.	Hostile fire is as follows:- "A" Battery were heavily shelled by a 7.7.mm. and a 10.5 c.m., several hits about dugouts and all round the guns, but no damage.	

Army Form C. 2118

WAR DIARY
or
INTELLIGENCE SUMMARY
(Erase heading not required.)

Instructions regarding War Diaries and Intelligence Summaries are contained in F. S. Regs., Part II. and the Staff Manual respectively. Title Pages will be prepared in manuscript.

Place	Date	Hour	Summary of Events and Information	Remarks and references to Appendices
In the Field.	April 29th	8.40.p.m.	HOSTILE FIRE - continued. X.30. was shelled by a 15.c.m. Battery suspected as being at T.20.a.	
"	"	7.30.am. to 9.13.am.	Battery positions at X.22.d.7½.0. and X.28.b.9.8. were heavily shelled by a 10.8.m. or 15.c.m. Battery, but the damage done was immaterial, as 5% are reported as blinds.	
"	"		Batteries of this Brigade expended 1728 A. 601.A.X.	
"	April 30th		Our Batteries did not fire much on this day.	
"	"	11.15 am. to 4.50.pm.	"A" Battery fired at enemy's front line trenches S.15.d.3.2½. - S.22.a.½.4½. in response to a call by the Infantry.	
"	"	4.35.pm.	Snipers plate or M.G. emplacement in enemy's front parapet in order to knock out loophole commanding suspected position of loaded mine, and to register enemy fron line. This was fired on by "C" Battery	
"	"	5.50.pm.	"D" Battery retaliated on the enemy's Trench Mortars.	
"	2	11.35 am. to 6.52.pm.	HOSTILE FIRE "A" Battery were shelled incessantly throughout the day by a 7.7.mm. Battery which fired 71 rounds, but caused no damage.	
			Ammunition expended by our Batteries were 44. A. 82. A.X.	

B. Buller
Lieut. Col. R.F.A.
Commanding 112th Brigade R.F.A.

112th. BRIGADE R. F. A.

25th. DIVISIONAL ARTILLERY

M A Y   1 9 1 6.

112th Bde. R.F.A.
(25th Div.)
May 1916

WAR DIARY or INTELLIGENCE SUMMARY

Army Form C. 2118

(Erase heading not required.)

Instructions regarding War Diaries and Intelligence Summaries are contained in F. S. Regs., Part II. and the Staff Manual respectively. Title Pages will be prepared in manuscript.

Place	Date	Hour	Summary of Events and Information	Remarks and references to Appendices
In the Field	May 1st.	4.35 p.m.	Batteries of this Brigade did not fire very much this day, but the enemy was very active. "A" Battery fired at trenches at S.15.d.3½.2.	
	"		"B" Battery did not fire.	
-do-	"		"C" Battery did not fire.	
	"	5.10.pm.	"D" Battery fired at Cross Roads for registration	
	"	1.14 a.m.	"D" Battery fired opp Trench 93 in response to S.O.S. Ammunition expended by Brigade 129 A. 35. A.X.	
			HOSTILE FIRE	
-do-	"	9.15 am.	"A" Battery XVIBM. was very heavily shelled by a 7.7.mm Gun reported to be at S.18.a.	
		4.44pm. to 5.p.m.	No damage was done. The Bethune Road also received some attention by a 7.7.mm. Gun Many other points were registered by the enemy with 7.7.mm. during the evening.	
-do-	May 2nd	9.20. a.m. &	"A" Battery fired at enemy's front line as they were worrying our Infantry.	
	"	4.10pm 6.40pm 6.50pm	"A" Battery fired at S.15.a.5.4. on orders from the Brigade Headquarters.	
	"	7.50.p.m.	"A" Battery fired at German Front line in retaliation for mine explosion.	
	2	8.p.m. to 1.30. a.m.	"B" Battery Barraged Enemy's Trenches.	
	"	11. am.	"C" Battery registered German Reserve Trenches	
		3.15.pm.	"C" Battery retaliated for Trench Mortars.	

Army Form C. 2118

WAR DIARY
or
INTELLIGENCE SUMMARY
(Erase heading not required.)

Instructions regarding War Diaries and Intelligence Summaries are contained in F. S. Regs., Part II. and the Staff Manual respectively. Title Pages will be prepared in manuscript.

Place	Date	Hour	Summary of Events and Information	Remarks and references to Appendices
In the Field.	May 2nd	5.pm. 7.57 p.m.	"C" Battery Enemy' support and reserve trenches. "C" Battery Barrage T.91 & T.90 in response to an S.O.S. Signal, a mine was sprung by the Germans, at first reported to be T.91. the T.90., then information was received that it was in T.89. Barrage was ordered by O.C. 112th Brigade.	
"		2.47. to 3.12. p.m.	"D" Battery registered loophole opposite Q.92.	
"		4.10 to 6.55. pm.	"D" Battery fired in retaliation for trench mortars opposite Q.91 and Q.93.	
"		8.3. to 8.53pm.	"D" Battery fired inretaliation for the mine that had been sprung by the Germans.	
"		9.27. to 12.46 p.m.	"D" Battery fired opposite Q.90 in order to annoy the enemy. Ammunition expended by the Brigade 1657 A. 270 A.X. HOSTILE FIRE	
"		9.a.m. to 7.30pm.	"A" Battery position was worried throughout this time by a 7.7.mmm Battery, but no damage was done.	
"		8.24 to 9.5.pm.	This Battery was again shelled by the 7.7.mm Battery, and no damage was caused this time. On the 1st and 2nd May the enemy pulled his balloon down at 3.p.m. On the 2nd May he again hoisted 2 balloons at 7.45.p.m., just prior to the explosion of their mine, from these they could undoubtedly spot our flashes.	

1875 Wt. W593/826 1,000,000 4/15 J.B.C. & A. A.D.S.S./Forms/C. 2118.

Army Form C. 2118

WAR DIARY
or
INTELLIGENCE SUMMARY
(Erase heading not required.)

Instructions regarding War Diaries and Intelligence
Summaries are contained in F.S. Regs., Part II.
and the Staff Manual respectively. Title Pages
will be prepared in manuscript.

Place	Date	Hour	Summary of Events and Information	Remarks and references to Appendices
In the Field.	May 3rd.	9.40. a.m.	"A" Battery fired at Whiz-bang Battery at S.18.2.1.2½. in retaliation for their intermittent fire on them.	
"	"	4.50. pm.	"A" Battery fired again in registration.	
"	"	9.10am.	"B" Battery fired in registration.	
"	"	4.55pm.	"B" Battery fired in retaliation for Trench Mortaring	
"	"	2.30pm	"C" Battery fired in retaliation on Trench Mortars over T.90.	
"	"	6.50pm.	"C" Battery again fired in retaliation for Trench Mortars over T.90 as they were greatly worrying our infantry.	
"	"	4.15.pm.	"C" Battery fired on Centre Crater T.90. 2 mines were sprung about 10° left of this Battery's zone. This Battery opened fire on Barrage "A" followed by Battery fire 10 secs. and then switched on to day lines when heavy enemy bombardment started there. After a short spell the Brigade Commander put them on to Barrage "A" again and then stopped.	
"	"	10.10. a.m. and 3.22pm.	"D" Battery registered craters.	
"	"	4.55pm. to 5.20pm.	"D" Battery Barrages Craters.	
"	"	7.43pm	"D" Battery again barraged craters.	
			HOSTILE FIRE	
"	"	4.55pm.	"A" Battery again received attention from the 7.7.mm Battery at S.18.a.12½. 30 rounds being fired. A direct hit on No. 3 Gun., killing the layer and wounding the No.1.	

Ammunition expended by our Batteries on this date was 412 A. 48 A.X.

Army Form C. 2118

WAR DIARY
or
INTELLIGENCE SUMMARY
(Erase heading not required.)

Instructions regarding War Diaries and Intelligence Summaries are contained in F. S. Regs., Part II. and the Staff Manual respectively. Title Pages will be prepared in manuscript.

Place	Date	Hour	Summary of Events and Information	Remarks and references to Appendices
In the field	May 4th	4.pm.	This was a very quiet day for Batteries of this Brigade as "A" "B" & "D" Batteries did not fire. "C" Battery ranged 2 guns on near lips of craters T.89 and L. of T.90 firing for effect on centre of crater. Evidently it was effective as the enemy retaliated. Ammunition expended 35. A. 20. A.X.	
"	"	4.15 6.30. & 7.25pm.	HOSTILE FIRE "D" Battery received some attention from a 7.7.mm. Battery suspected to be at GIVENCHY. "A" Battery were fired at by a 10.5.c.m. Battery, but no damage was done in either case.	
"	May 5th.		INTELLIGENCE At 7.48.p.m. a green light was observed to go up behind BERTHONVAL WOOD, line passing through X.29.b.8½.5½. At 8.57 this was repeated. At 3.a.m. A mine reported as having gone up on the right about 51st Div. Area. It has been noticed that during the lasr few days the shooting done by the enemy's anti-Aircraft guns has been remarkably bad. Their fuze setting particularly erratic. About 50 shells fired at our aircraft on the 3rd and 4th burst on graze round about BERTHONVAL WOOD. The enemy's Trench Mortars have been very active and are a great source of trouble to our Infantry. Much retaliation for these are required from this Brigade.	
"	"	7.30pm. 12.15 to 1.p.m.	"A" Battery fired at S.15.d.8½.1. to S.22.a.1.6. in response to an S.O.S. from Infantry.	
"	"	6.5. to 9.p.m.	"B" Battery fired in retaliation.	
"	"		"B" Battery Barraged Q.90 with 211 rounds.	
"	"	4.30 to 6.p.m.	"C" Battery registered all guns on front parapet of crater at S.15.d.7830.	

Army Form C. 2118

WAR DIARY
or
INTELLIGENCE-SUMMARY

(Erase heading not required.)

Instructions regarding War Diaries and Intelligence Summaries are contained in F. S. Regs., Part II. and the Staff Manual respectively. Title Pages will be prepared in manuscript.

Place	Date	Hour	Summary of Events and Information	Remarks and references to Appendices
In the field Continued				
"	May 5th	5.30pm. 7.23 to 7.26p.m.	"C" Battery fired at Crater T.89. "C" Battery fired (T.89., T.90.) as enemy were attacking. Infantry reported fire was very effective, Enemy parapet much knocked about	
"	"	7.26 to 8.56pm.	"D" Battery barraged opposite T.90. Ammunition expended by the Brigade was 1178 A. 65. A.X.	
"	"		HOSTILE FIRE	
"	"	7.30. to 8.30pm.	The enemy heavily shelled "A" Battery with 7.7.mm gun, 174 rounds being fired.	
"	"	1.p.m. to 4.p.m.	"B" Battery received some attention from a 15 cm. How. about 100 rounds No damage.	
"	"	8.p.m. to 9.p.m.	"C" Battery received attention from a 4.2" How and 7.7.mm in retaliation for their firing.	
"	May 6th	11.am. & 1pm.	"A" Battery registered the enemys front line from a new position. "C" & "D" Batteries fired a few round in registration. Ammunition expended by the Brigade 31 A. There was no hostile fire on this day.	
"	May 7th		This was also a very quiet day the Batteries firing very little and receiving very little attention from the Hun. The Brigade retaliated on the enemy's Trench Mortars. Ammunition expended by the Brigade 82 A. 21.A.X.	
"	"	10.30.am. to 12.25pm.	HOSTILE FIRE was directed against "C" Battery, but no damage was done. 70 rounds.	

Army Form C. 2118

WAR DIARY
or
INTELLIGENCE SUMMARY
(Erase heading not required.)

Instructions regarding War Diaries and Intelligence Summaries are contained in F.S. Regs., Part II. and the Staff Manual respectively. Title Pages will be prepared in manuscript.

Place	Date	Hour	Summary of Events and Information	Remarks and references to Appendices
In the Field	May 8th	1.44pm. to 9.30.pm.	Batteries of the Brigade retaliated for enemy's trench Mortars, Craters Q.89/3 , Q.90/2 were also registered by them. The road from GIVENCHY to AVION was fired on as a likely spot for enemy's transport. Mines were sprung in the 7th Brigade area about 8.p.m. Ammunition expended by the Brigade 280 A. 87 A.X.	
"	"	6.pm. to 6.40.pm.	HOSTILE FIRE "A" Battery was shelled by a 7.7.mm Battery	
"	May 9th	8.30am. to 9.40.pm.	Retaliation on enemy's Trench Mortars, Mine sprung by the enemy Left of T.90. at 7.47.p.m. Batteries at once opened fire in support of the Infantry fighting for the crater. Barrage on the enemy's communication trenches was kept up by the Brigade until about 9.50.p.m. Communications throughout held good. Ammunition expended by the Brigade 1578. A. 124 A.X.	
"	"	8.30pm.	HOSTILE FIRE:- 6 rounds on the BETHUNE ROAD S.19.d.	
"	May 10th	10.30.am. to 7.30.p.m.	The day was very quiet and the Batteries of this Brigade did not fire a great deal "C" Battery registered with kite balloon at 6.20.p.m. Batteries retaliated and also fired in order to catch working parties probably working behind Q.89/3 Crater. The telephonic communication which now exists across the ZOUAVE VALLEY is satisfactory The work of placing it over wire netting was done with the assistance of the LOYAL NORTH LANCS.	
"	"	8.30.am. & 3.30.pm.	HOSTILE FIRE:- The enemy fired 18 rounds at the BETHUNE ROAD, these rounds gave off issue of green smoke on bursting. Ammunitin fired by the Brigade 119 A. 19. A.X.	
"	May 11th	10.55 am. to 1.45pm.	Batteries of this Brigade retaliated for Trench Mortars, registered Crater 89/3 The day was very quiet on our Sector. Ammunition expended 138 A. 45 A.X.	
"	"	2.pm. to 6.pm.	HOSTILE FIRE:- A hostile Battery suspected as being E. of LA FOLIE WOOD fired about 250 rounds, at a Battery in the Centre Sector.	

Army Form C. 2118

WAR DIARY
~~INTELLIGENCE SUMMARY~~
(Erase heading not required.)

Instructions regarding War Diaries and Intelligence Summaries are contained in F. S. Regs., Part II. and the Staff Manual respectively. Title Pages will be prepared in manuscript.

Place	Date	Hour	Summary of Events and Information	Remarks and references to Appendices
In The Field	May 12th	9.20.am. to 7.p.m.	The day was quiet, Batteries of this Brigade fired in retaliation for Trench Mortars also on the enemy's Support Trenches. A suspicious sheet of sacking puckered to look like the sand bags surrounding it can be detected at N.W. corner of Q.89/3 Crater, probably it must hide a Machine Gun. Ammunition expended by the Brigade 109 A. 36. A.X. HOSTILE FIRE :- There has been no hostile fire to-day, but the enemy has closely registered S.25.a.8.5., at this point duck boards from St.ELOI cross the BETHUNE ROAD.	
"	May 13th	2.20.pm. to 9.25.pm.	Batteries fired in retaliation also in support. The enemy sprung a mine, but the exact location was not reported. Batteries of the Brigade Barraged trenches Opposite 87/88. Ammunition expended :- 1511 A. 305 A.X.	
"			HOSTILE FIRE :- NIL.	
"	May 14th	2.51 am. to 6.15.pm.	The Brigade fired during the day at suspected Trench Mortar Batteries at S.16.c.3.5. - S.15.d.20.47. - S.15.c.80.85. - S.16.c.40.25. - S.16.c.51. in retaliation for them annoying our Infantry. Ammunituon expended :- 253 A. 97 A.X.	
"		3.30pm. to 6.pm.	HOSTILE FIRE. "A" Battery were shelled by a 5.9 c.m. during this time with no results. 60 rounds.	
"	May 15th	7.50.am, to 11.55.pm.	Batteries carried out retaliation for trench mortars during the day. At about 8.30.p.m. Mines were sprung by our Infantry, the enemy immediately opened a heavy barrage on our trenches within 10 secs of the mines going up. Rockets giving a pair of red lights were sent up by the enemy's Infantry this apparently being a call for artillery support. Communications were perfect throughout the "Straffe" and lamp signalling was established. Ammunition expended:- 1839 A. 358 A.X.	
"	May 16th	Various. 12.10pm. to 6.5. p.m.	Batteries were engaged in minor operations on barraged points ordered from time to time also retaliation for Trench Mortars. Ammunition expended :- 282 A. 239 A.X. HOSTILE FIRE:- NIL.	

Army Form C. 2118

WAR DIARY
or
INTELLIGENCE SUMMARY
(Erase heading not required.)

Instructions regarding War Diaries and Intelligence Summaries are contained in F. S. Regs., Part II. and the Staff Manual respectively. Title Pages will be prepared in manuscript.

Place	Date	Hour	Summary of Events and Information	Remarks and references to Appendices
In the Field	May 17th	8.5.pm. to 9.45.pm.	Batteries of the Brigade fired on Crater 89/3, 88/1, also registered points on the enemy's front. "C" Battery retaliated on S.15.central - S.15.d.4.7., S.15.d.55. - S.16.c.0.1. "D" Battery carried out an intermittent barrage between 11.26.a.m. and 3.47.p.m. & 6.41pm. Retaliation for Trench Mortars were also carried out. to 8.p.m. Ammunition expended:- 1633 A. 1212 A.X.	
"	"	2.45. to 5.p.m.	HOSTILE FIRE:- "A" Battery's new position received a good deal of attention 115.rounds 8" and 5.9. Crater 88/1 and support trenches also received some attention with 13.c.m. 10.c.m. and 7.7.mm. Heavy barrage was also carried out on our trenches during the day.	
"	May 18th	10.am. to 10.am. 19th.	The Brigade registered various points on the enem's front, also retaliated on enemy' Trench Mortars. There was a minor operation on crater 81. during 12.15. pm. to 3.30.pm. Suspected positions of Trench Mortars were also registered. Ammunition expended:- 394 A. 99. A.X.	
"	May 19th	10.am. to 10.am. 20th	HOSTILE FIRE:- During the period of report the enemy intermittently barraged our trenches in front of crater Q.88/1 and also Q.89 trench, Our Batteries were not shelled. Enemy's aircraft were very active. Batteries of the Brigade registered the enemy's trenches, suspected Trench Mortar Batteries also crater on Central Bde. Front. German trenches and emplacements were also shelled. Retaliation was also called for by the Infantry on the enemy's Trench Mortars.	
"	May 20th	10.am. to 10am 21st	Hostile Fire:- The enemy was a little active to-day shelling "A" Battery's position also "D" Battery with 5.9" and 4.2", suspected positions were at S.23.d.5.3. and VIMY. The enemy also opened a very heavy barrage on our right, continueing for about 30 minutes. "B" Battery also received some attention, there communications were severed from B.H.Q. but these were soon repaired. (No. of rounds fired by the enemy about 48.) Ammunition expended by this Brigade 181 A. 108 A.X.	

Army Form C. 2118

WAR DIARY
or
INTELLIGENCE-SUMMARY

(Erase heading not required.)

Instructions regarding War Diaries and Intelligence Summaries are contained in F.S. Regs., Part II. and the Staff Manual respectively. Title Pages will be prepared in manuscript.

Place	Date	Hour	Summary of Events and Information	Remarks and references to Appendices
In the Field	May 20th	10.a.m. to 10.a.m 21st.	"B" and "D" Batteries of this Brigade did not fire. "A" Battery registered various points on their zone. "C" Battery retaliated on the enemy's Trench Mortars which were greatly annoying our Infantry. This Battery reports that it was particularly noticeable on this day the superiority of the enemy's TRENCH MORTARS to those of ours. Ammunition expended:- 684 A. 598. A.X.	
In the Field	May 21st	10.a.m.	HOSTILE FIRE:-) The enemy was very active during the day "A" Battery being heavily shelled by a 5.9", also X.23.d. was shelled by a 10.5. or 15 cm. Trench Mortaring along our line Q.86., 87., and 88, receiving most attention. Early on the 21st the enemy began to heavily shell our Batteries, and "D" Battery had a direct hit on the gun pit where the ammunition was stacked, destroying 103 A. & 17.A.X. The Batteries of this Brigade were heavily shelled all through the day, causing a great many casualties. Gas, tear shells were used by the enemy during this bombardment. Communications between the Batteries and Brigade Headquarters were being continually cut by hostile fire, but these were soon repaired by the linesmen of this Brigade. Brigade Headquarters came out of forward position and returned to VILLERS AU BOIS on the night of 22nd, this relief should have been carried out on the night of 21st, but owing to the activity of the enemy the relief was cancelled.	
"	May 22nd	2 "	Brigade Headquarters moved to VILLERS AU BOIS, and relief of Batteries by the 47th Divisional Artillery was completed that night, with the exception of "A" Battery who remained in action under orders of the 47th until 27th May 1916.	
	May 23rd to 24th		Brigade Headquarters at VILLERS AU BOIS and 3 Batteries at wagon lines. General duties were carried out.	
"	May 25th		Brigade Headquarters moved from VILLERS AU BOIS to wagon line at CAMBLIGNEUL.	

Army Form C. 2118

WAR DIARY
or
INTELLIGENCE SUMMARY

(Erase heading not required.)

Instructions regarding War Diaries and Intelligence Summaries are contained in F. S. Regs., Part II. and the Staff Manual respectively. Title Pages will be prepared in manuscript.

Place	Date	Hour	Summary of Events and Information	Remarks and references to Appendices
In the Field.	May 26th		3 Batteries and Brigade Headquarters at Wagon lines. General duties carried out.	
	May 27th		Brigade Ammunition Column passed under command of O.C. No 3 Section 25th D.A.C. Brigade Headquarters and 3 Batteries carried out general duties. "A" Battery came out of action.	
"	May 28th		Brigade Headquarters and 4 Batteries at wagon lines. General Duties carried out.	
"	May 29th		General Duties carried out by the Brigade at Wagon lines.	
	May 30th.		Brigade Headquarters and Batteries moved from Cambligneul to Camp at St Michel leaving Cambligneul at various times.	
	May 31st		Brigade at Camp, STM MICHEL, General duties carried out arranging camp and generally tidying up.	

[signature]
Lieut. Col. R.F.A.
Commanding 112th Brigade R.F.A.

25th. DIVISIONAL ARTILLERY

112th. BRIGADE R. F. A.

25th. DIVISIONAL ARTILLERY

JUNE 1916.

Army Form C. 2118.

June

112-RFA Vol 8

XXV

WAR DIARY
or
~~INTELLIGENCE~~ SUMMARY

(Erase heading not required.)

Instructions regarding War Diaries and Intelligence Summaries are contained in F.S. Regs., Part II. and the Staff Manual respectively. Title Pages will be prepared in manuscript.

Place	Date	Hour	Summary of Events and Information	Remarks and references to Appendices
ST. MICHEL	1st June 1916		3 Batteries and Brigade Headquarters in Rest area at ST. MICHEL. (Divisional Scheme at training area. General Duties carried out.	
-do-	2nd June		General Training by 3 Batteries and Brigade Headquarters at Training area.	
-do-	3rd June		General Duties and Training by 3 Batteries and Brigade Headquarters at Training Area.	
-do-	4th June		General Duties and Training at St. MICHEL by 3 Batteries and Brigade Headquarters.	
-do-	5th June		3 Batteries and Brigade Headquarters at St. MICHEL - General Training and Duties.	
-do-	6th June		3 Batteries and Brigade Headquarters - Divisional Scheme in Training area - Weather Wet.	
-do-	7th June		3 Batteries and B.H.Q. - General Duties and Training in Training area.	
-do-	8th June		3 Batteries and Brigade Headquarters - Divisional Tactical Scheme - Training Area.	
-do-	9th June		3 Batteries and Brigade Headquarters - General Duties in Rest Area.	
-do-	10th June		3 Batteries and Brigade Headquarters - General Duties at Rest Area.	

2449 Wt. W14957/Mg0 750,000 1/16 J.B.C. & A. Forms/C.2118/12.

Army Form C. 2118

WAR DIARY
or
INTELLIGENCE-SUMMARY
(Erase heading not required.)

Instructions regarding War Diaries and Intelligence Summaries are contained in F. S. Regs., Part II. and the Staff Manual respectively. Title Pages will be prepared in manuscript.

Place	Date	Hour	Summary of Events and Information	Remarks and references to Appendices
St. Michel	11th June		General Duties at Rest Area. - 3 Batteries and Brigade Headquarters - Church Parade.	
-do-	12th June		3 Batteries and Brigade Headquarters - Training Area - Practice for Divisional Scheme.	
-do-	13th June		3 Batteries and Brigade Headquarters - Training Area - Divisional Tactical Scheme - Received orders to move to ----------	
-do-	14th June		3 Batteries and Brigade Headquarters - General Duties in Camp at ST MICHEL.	
-do-	15th June		3 Batteries and Brigade Headquarters Moved from St. Michel to Occoches where they remained in billets, awaiting further orders.	
OCCOCHES	16th June		General Duties at OCCOCHES - Received orders to move to M---------- on the following night.	
-do-	17th June		General Cleaning up at OCCOCHES - 3 Batteries and Brigade Headquarters moved at night to MONTRELET. - 2 Officers and 23 other ranks of the W/25 T.M. Battery joined the Brigade.	
MONTRELET	18th June		3 Batteries and Brigade Headquarters at MONTRELET - Colonel and Battery Commanders went forward to reconnoitre.	
-do-	19th June		3 Batteries and Brigade Headquarters at MONTRELET - Colonel, Adjutant, and Battery Commanders went forward to reconnoitre.	

Army Form. C. 2118

WAR DIARY
or
INTELLIGENCE-SUMMARY
(Erase heading not required.)

Instructions regarding War Diaries and Intelligence Summaries are contained in F.S. Regs., Part II. and the Staff Manual respectively. Title Pages will be prepared in manuscript.

Place	Date	Hour	Summary of Events and Information	Remarks and references to Appendices
MONTRELET	20th June		C.R.A., 25th Divisional Artillery inspected 3 Batteries and Brigade Headquarters, Horses, vehicles, and men at MONTRELET - "D" Battery (Howitzer) rejoined the Brigade from the line after attachment to the 51st D.A. Lieut. P.L. Jones - 2nd Lieut. Lane.- 2nd Lieut. Durnford joined the Brigade.	
-do-	21st June		Batteries and Brigade Headquarters at MONTRELET - General Duties and Training were carried out.	
-do-	22nd June.		Batteries and Brigade Headquarters at Montrelet - General Duties werex carried out.	
-do-	23rd June		Batteries and Brigade Headquarters at MONTRELET - G.O.C.,R.A. inspected "D" Battery at MONTRELET. General Duties were carried out.	
-do-	24th June		Brigade at MONTRELET - General Training and Duties carried out.	
-do-	25th June.		Brigade at MONTRELET - General Duties and Trainxxxxxixxxxxx Training carried out.	
-do-	26th June.		Brigade at MONTRELET - Adjutant and other Officers went forward to reconnoitre - G.O.C.,R.A. inspected the Brigade at the Training Area.	
-do-	27th June.		Brigade at MONTRELET - Received orders for the Brigade to move to --------- the following day. Captain C.H. Fraser transferred from "A" Battery to command the No.1. Section of the 25th D.A.C.	
-do-	28th June.		Brigade marched from MONTRELET to HARPONVILLE - Brigade Headquarters leading followed by Batteries at ½ hour intervals (distance of journey about 14½ miles) Brigade arrived in Billets at HARPONVILLE, and awaited further orders. (very wet)	

Army Form C. 2118.

WAR DIARY
or
INTELLIGENCE SUMMARY

(Erase heading not required.)

Instructions regarding War Diaries and Intelligence Summaries are contained in F. S. Regs., Part II. and the Staff Manual respectively. Title Pages will be prepared in manuscript.

Place	Date	Hour	Summary of Events and Information	Remarks and references to Appendices
HARPONVILLE	29th June		The Brigade at HARPONVILLE - General Duties carried out. The G.O.C. Division and G.O.C.,R.A. visited the Brigade.	
-do-	30th June		General Duties at HARPONVILLE - 15 O.R. Received for the Brigade also 20 Remounts.	

(signature)

Lieut. Col. R.F.A.
Commanding 112th Brigade R.F.A.

2449 Wt. W14957/M90 750,000 1/16 J.B.C. & A. Forms/C.2118/12.

25th Div.

WAR DIARY

Headquarters,

112th BRIGADE, R.F.A.

J U L Y

1 9 1 6

Army Form C.2118.

WAR DIARY or INTELLIGENCE-SUMMARY

(Erase heading not required.)

VOLUME II
112 Brigade R.F.A.
Vol 9

Instructions regarding War Diaries and Intelligence Summaries are contained in F.S. Regs., Part II and the Staff Manual respectively. Title Pages will be prepared in manuscript.

Place	Date	Hour	Summary of Events and Information	Remarks and references to Appendices
HARPONVILLE	1st July 1916		Brigade at Harponville. Received orders at 9.p.m. to march out of present billets. Brigade Marched out at 9.30.p.m. and proceeded to VADENCOURT Wood; Brigade camped here and awaited further orders.	
VADENCOURT	2nd.		Brigade at VADENCOURT - General Duties and training carried out.	
-do-	3rd		Brigade still camping at VADENCOURT - Adjutant and Battery Commanders went forward to the firing line. Received orders to stand by to relieve the 32nd Division.	
-do-	4th		Brigade at VADENCOURT - Colonel and 2nd Lieut. Nowell-Usticke go forward next to the firing line. Orders received cancelling the relieve of the 32nd Division.	
-do-	5th		Brigade at Vadencourt - Colonel, Adjutant, and Battery Commanders still forward. Orders received for the Brigade to move, Batteries to go into action and the Wagon Line area to be in the vicinity of BOUZINCOURT. Right Section of "B" Battery transferred to "A" Battery, and Left Section to "C" Battery. Brigade Headquarters moved off at 7.p.m. followed by Batteries at intervals.	
Inc See Field	6th		Brigade in action - Batteries registered various parts of the enemy's front.	
-do-	7th		Heavy Bombardment on our right by our own guns - Enemy's S.O.S. Signals very numerous, but their retaliation very feeble.	
		7.30.am.	A cloud of browny white cylinder gas was being liberated from (roughly about X.2.a.) Drifting North Westwards.	
-do-	8th		Situation normal on the 112th Brigade front - An hostile Observation balloon was reported to be 91° 30" right of MARTINSART CHURCH from W.9.d.7.6. also true bearing 54° 40" from W.18.d.9.9.	
-do-	9th	4.a.m.	Situation normal on the Brigade Front. -	
		8.55am.	Bombarded Trenches X.2.a. & c.	
		4.25pm.	Heavy Hostile shelling S.E. of OVILLERS - Volumes of dense black smoke were seen at 4.5.p.m.	

Army Form C. 2118.

WAR DIARY
or
INTELLIGENCE SUMMARY

(Erase heading not required.)

Instructions regarding War Diaries and Intelligence Summaries are contained in F. S. Regs., Part II. and the Staff Manual respectively. Title Pages will be prepared in manuscript.

Place	Date	Hour	Summary of Events and Information	Remarks and references to Appendices
In The Field	9th continued	4.25pm.	issuing from POZIERES thought to be caused by our heavies firing from MARTINSART - Otherwise situation obscure.	
-do-	10th	3.45am.	Situation normal on the 112th Brigade front.	
		10.25am.	An enemy working party was seen on crest line 1° 20' left of COURCELETTE Chimney. - Continued Barrage with occasional bursts at MOUQUET FARM to stop movement there.	
		4.pm.	Situation unchanged on the Brigade front. Two Hostile Balloons up all day.	
-do-	11th		Hostile Kite Balloons up in same place as yesterday. Situation normal on the Brigade front. Batteries registered various points on their zone.	
-do-	12th to 12th	12 noon 12 noon	Batteries registered New Targets. - German Working party observed at X.2.a.3.2., these were dispersed by 2 Battery salvos from "A" Battery. 2 German Red Cross men walked out into the open at X.a.c.5.5. and carried a wounded man into the trench. - The trench is very badly knocked about as the men were walking on the top most of the way. 3 Hostile Observation Balloons observed, Bearing from W.15.a.5.6. :- 69° , 52°30'', 78°30'' Hostile fire NIL.	
-do-	12th to 13th.	12 noon noon	The enemy's support and communication trenches and Tramway were shelled during the day by "C" Battery. "A" Battery barraged N. of OVILLERS in support of the attack between 11.p.m. and 1.a.m. "D" Battery registered various points on the enemy's front. The enemy shelled AUTHUILLE WOOD at 12 noon on the 12th the nature of the gun used was a 10.c.m. and 7.7.mm. 110 rounds were fired.	
-do-	13th to 12 noon 14th.	12 noon	Batteries of the Brigade barraged the enemy's Trenches in support of Infantry operation N. of OVILLERS. - 2046 rounds of Ammunition expended. The enemy fired 1 round of 5.9" at "D" Battery, but no damage was done. The enemy also shelled AVELUY with a 15.c.m. Gun, and AUTHUILLE Wood with a 7.7.mm Gun. The German put up a number of white lights from West of OVILLERS at 6.a.m. - No visible action followed - Weather Misty.	

Army Form C. 2118.

WAR DIARY
or
INTELLIGENCE SUMMARY

(Erase heading not required.)

Instructions regarding War Diaries and Intelligence Summaries are contained in F. S. Regs., Part II. and the Staff Manual respectively. Title Pages will be prepared in manuscript.

Place	Date	Hour	Summary of Events and Information	Remarks and references to Appendices
In the Field.	14th to 15th.	12 noon to 12 noon	A continuous barrage of the enemy's front, support, and communication trenches was carried out. - 2558 rounds of ammunition was used. A party of about 15 Germans were seen to leave a trench about 4.45.p.m. - They were at once fired upon by an 18 pdr Battery and then disappeared. The enemy fired 1 round of 4.2" H.E. every 10 minutes during the day on CUNISTON STREET between CUNISTON POST and WENNING STREET.	
-do-	15th to 16th.	12 noon to 12 noon	Batteries of this Brigade, Barraged and Registered various points on their zone. "A" Battery also engaged fleeting targets. Number of rounds fired 2579. There was no Hostile fire to report. - Weather clear.	
-do-	16th to 17th.	12 noon to 12 noon	Batteries of this Brigade Barraged, and Registered many enemy's points on their zone. The Hun fired about 20 rounds at X.1.a.7.3. between 5.p.m. and 5.5.p.m. on the 16th. The Infantry of the 32nd Division and the 97th Brigade were relieved by the 144th Brigade A quiet day.	
-do-	17th to 18th.	12 noon to 12 noon	"A" Battery of this Brigade did not fire owing to changing Battery position as ordered. The remaining Batteries fired at enemy's trenches and other targets. The enemy heavily shelled CONTALMAISON and SAUSAGE VALLEY at N.E. end. A number of gas and Lacrymatory shell were fired during the night. "C" Battery's position was also shelled by the enemy between the hours of 3.p.m. and 10.pm. about 10 rounds of 7.7.mm. and 10.5.c.m. being fired.	
-do-	18th to 19th.	12 noon to 12 noon	"A" Battery barraged on main trench W. of POZIERES. "C" Battery barraged X.3.c. in support of the Infantry. "D" Battery fired at POZIERE WINDMILL. and trench X.4.a. and X.4.c. with very satisfactory results. The Hun fired between 50 and 60 rounds at "C" Battery's position, the majority of the shell fell in the open ground in front of the position. SAUSAGE VALLEY AND MASH VALLEY were also shelled during the day.	

Army Form C. 2118.

WAR DIARY
or
INTELLIGENCE SUMMARY
(Erase heading not required.)

Instructions regarding War Diaries and Intelligence Summaries are contained in F.S. Regs., Part II. and the Staff Manual respectively. Title Pages will be prepared in manuscript.

Place	Date	Hour	Summary of Events and Information	Remarks and references to Appendices
In the Field.	19th to 20th.	12 noon to 12 noon	Infantry Reliefs carried out under cover of dark. 112th Brigade:- 1 18 pdr Battery ordered to fire on intermediate trench from X.4.c.5.9. - R.34.c.3.1. commencing at 9.p.m. 1 18 pdr Battery ordered to fire 40 rounds an hour into POZIERES till further orders.	
-do-	20th to 21st.	12 noon to 12 noon	Brigade carried out instructions as ordered in 12th Divisional Artillery operation order No 14	
-do-	21st.	10am.	The 25th Divisional Artillery Group, consisting of the 110th 111th, and 112th Brigades R.F.A. became the Corps Artillery and placed at the disposal of the G.O.C. Xth Corps for special tasks in the OVILLERS and POZIERES Sector. In the event of a hostile attack on our Salient South of POZIERES the following task was allotted :- 112th Brigade will sweep the road from :- X.4.b.7.2. to X.5.a.3.7. and the Railway from X.5.a.1.5. to X.5.a.9.5.	
-do-	22nd		Wire cutting carried out by b the Brigade and 400 rounds per 24 hours enfilading trenches in X.2.a. and X.2.b. This task was carried out until further Orders. Reference Xth Corps (25th Divisional Artillery) Artillery Operation Order No 38 the following tasks were ordered:- 2 18 pdr batteries to barrage the length of road between X.4.b.8.3. and X.5.a.3.7. - Barrage to extend to 75 yards on either side of the road. 2 18 pdr batteries to form a barrage 100 yards for a length of 200 yards from X.4.c.7.8. to X.4.b.2.2. Ammunition H.E. only. O.C. 112th Brigade will keep one section in OVILLERS in observation for the special purposes of dealing with :- Counter Attack, - Movements of parties of the enemy N. of POZIERES.	
-do-	Night of 22/23rd.		The Brigade barraged points in support of the Infantry attack which was being carried out. "D" Battery barraged the trench from X.4.c.6.5. to X.4.c.7.8. - 2 Batteries of The Brigade barraged from X.4.b.8.3. to X.5.a.3.7. also from X.4.b.7.6. to X.5.a.3.7. Heavy Shelling of POZIERES reported.	
	24th			
-do-	25th	3.30.a.m.	The 1st Australian Division continue their attack Northwards through POZIERES - Brigade barraged from 3.a.m. to 5.a.m. "A" Battery ordered to fire Centre Section at WINDMILL in R.35.c. which is armed with a machine gun. - 2nd Lieut. Lane sent to G.O.C. 1st Australian	

2449 Wt. W14957/M90 750,000 1/16 J.B.C. & A. Forms/C.2118/12.

Army Form C. 2118.

WAR DIARY
or
INTELLIGENCE SUMMARY

(Erase heading not required.)

Instructions regarding War Diaries and Intelligence Summaries are contained in F. S. Regs., Part II. and the Staff Manual respectively. Title Pages will be prepared in manuscript.

Place	Date	Hour	Summary of Events and Information	Remarks and references to Appendices
In the Field.	25th	Cont:	1st Australian Brigade as Liaison Officer with instructions to keep H.Q., R.A. informed of the progress of the attack. Batteries ordered to man their O.P.'s continuously day and night until further orders.	
		7.40.a.m.	Liaison Officer reports 7.25.a.m. enemy directing very heavy fire on X.4. — POZIERES shrouded in smoke — Fire from N.E. of Field Guns 5.9" or heavier.	
	Night of 25th/26th		1st Australian Division carried out reliefs under cover of darkness. Brigade ordered to shell a line joining the undermentioned points :— R.34.d.9.7. — R.35.c.2.6. — R.35.a.9.0. Fire to commence at 9.30.p.m. and continue until 12.30.a.m. — To re-open at 2.a.m. and continue until 4.a.m.	
	Night of 28/29th		The 2nd Australian Division attacked the German position N. and N.E. of POZIERES. The 18 pdrs of the Brigade were ordered to shell the track from R.34.b.5.5. to R.29.b. with shrapnel and H.E. The Barrages as carried out on the night of the 26th to be carried out commencing at 9.15.p.m.	
-do-	30th	Various.	Batteries of the Brigade Registered, and Barraged various points on the enemy's front to stop wire being put up and also to stop working parties.	
-do-	31st	-do-	The enemy's front was closely registered and barraged by Batteries in order to stop working parties. Mash Valley was shelled during the morning.	

P Parker
Lieut. Col. R.F.A.
Commanding 112th Brigade R.F.A.

25th Divisional Artillery.

112th BRIGADE.

ROYAL FIELD ARTILLERY.

AUGUST 1 9 1 6

Army Form C. 2118.

112 Bde R.F.A. Vol 10

WAR DIARY
or
INTELLIGENCE-SUMMARY

(Erase heading not required.)

Instructions regarding War Diaries and Intelligence Summaries are contained in F. S. Regs., Part II. and the Staff Manual respectively. Title Pages will be prepared in manuscript.

Place	Date	Hour	Summary of Events and Information	Remarks and references to Appendices
In the Field.	Aug: 1st to 3rd.	Various.	The Brigade carried out day and night barrages on the enemy's communications	
	3/4th		Supported the 12th Divisional attack on German Line running from OVILLERS to POZIERES.	
	4th		Last nights attack successful. - Supported 2nd Australian Division who attacked German 1st and 2nd line trenches N.E. & E. of OVILLERS at 9.p.m.	
	5th		Last nights attack successful. - Resume barrages on enemy's communications.	
	6th to 8th		Normal barrages kept up.- On night of the 8th supported 4th Australian Division who attacked enemy's defences North of POZIERES. C/112 move to new position 300 yards west of CONTALMAISON on night of 7th.	
	9th		Objective last night secured. - Supported 4th Australian Division who continue their attack to-night at midnight.	
	10th & 11th		Usual day and night barrages and moving targets engaged.	
	12th		Supported 4th Australian Division who attack enemy's positions around MOUQUET FARM.	
	13th		Enemy retook positions captured by us yesterday. - Germans had 6 - 7 balloons up this is very unusual.	
	14th		The Brigade supported Australians in Minor Operations.	

Army Form C. 2118.

WAR DIARY
or
INTELLIGENCE SUMMARY
(Erase heading not required.)

Instructions regarding War Diaries and Intelligence Summaries are contained in F. S. Regs, Part II. and the Staff Manual respectively. Title Pages will be prepared in manuscript.

Place	Date	Hour	Summary of Events and Information	Remarks and references to Appendices
In the FIELD.	14th contin.		Heavy firing through night. - Enemy made counter attack.	
	15th		Supported 48th Divn. who continued their attack at 12.15.a.m. on 15/16th.	
	16th &		Lasts nights attack not successful. - On night of 16th Brigade took over 4 18 pdrs from 48th Divn.	
	17th		Day and night barrages kept up.	
	18th		Enemy's artillery was very active during the preceeding 24 hours. Brigade supported the 48th Divn, who continued their attack at 5.p.m. This attack was very successfully carried out.	
	19th & 20th		Night barrages kept up - A certain amount of activity during the day. Captain H.J. Vincent transferred from the Brigade to the 111th Brigade to Command "C" Battery 111th Bde. R.F.A. - 19.8.16.	
	21st		Brigade supported 48th Division who continued their attack at 6.p.m. and which proved very successful.	
	22nd.		Enemy Artillery very active throughout the day. Their Infantry make an attack on 48th Division, but are repulsed. Night firing as usual.	
	23rd.		Normal day - Nothing to report.	
	24th		Supported 25th Divisional Artillery who attack South of THEIPVAL at 4.p.m. This attack was very successfully carried out.	
	25th		The enemy are very active throughout the day - They make a counter attack during the afternoon, but are repulsed. Another counter attack was made by the enemy during the night 25/26th, this also being repulsed.	

2449 Wt. W14957/Mgo 750,000 1/16 J.B.C. & A. Forms/C.2118/12.

Army Form C. 2118.

WAR DIARY
or
INTELLIGENCE SUMMARY
(Erase heading not required.)

Instructions regarding War Diaries and Intelligence Summaries are contained in F. S. Regs., Part II and the Staff Manual respectively. Title Pages will be prepared in manuscript.

Place	Date	Hour	Summary of Events and Information	Remarks and references to Appendices
In The Field.	26th		Normal conditions.	
	27th		25th Division take over line held by 48th Division. 112th Brigade R.F.A. cover Right Infantry Brigade (74th) Support attack of 48th Division carried out at 7.p.m.	
	28th		The Brigade moved and took over new positions, close to ATHUILLE WOOD, from 48th Division. We do not take part in the attack carried out by the 75th Infantry Bde to-day.	
	29th		Enemy Artillery very active. - Night barrages kept up.	
	30th		A very wet day - Things fairly quiet - Barrages at night as usual.	
	31st.		Normal day.	

Lieut. Col. R.F.A.
Commanding 112th Brigade R.F.A.

25th. DIVISION
ARTILLERY

112th. BRIGADE R. F. A.

25th. DIVISIONAL ARTILLERY

SEPTEMBER 1916.

Army Form C. 2118

vol 11
112 RFA

WAR DIARY
or
INTELLIGENCE SUMMARY
(Erase heading not required.)

Place	Date	Hour	Summary of Events and Information	Remarks and references to Appendices
In the Field.	Sept. 1st.		Registration by Batteries. -- Several small parties of Germans were fired at by batteries throughout the day.	
	2nd.		Registrations carried out by Batteries for an attack to be carried out on the 3rd inst. Brigade fire several salvos on working party around old well. Enemy shell AUTHUILLE WOOD, Tramway Corner, and around "C" Battery position during the afternoon.	
	3rd.		The Brigade supported the 75th Brigade who attacked South of THIEPVAL at 5.10. a.m. This attack was unsuccessful. Hostile movements noticed throughout the day around the WONDER WORK. Bursts of fire of 50 rounds or more were put in or around this place during the day. Enemy Artillery active. -- Night firing :- "A" Battery fire 35 rounds per hour on WONDER WORK, "D" Battery 15 rounds per hour around the well throughout the night.	
	4th.		Registration carried out by all Batteries, many good moving targets engaged. Night firing as for last night carried out by "B" and "D" Batteries. "D" Battery also fire occasional rounds into COURCELETTE.	
	5th.		Enemy movements fired on with observed fire throughout the day, the vicinity of the well receiving special attention. Enemy put a heavy barrage on our left Battalion shortly after 10.p.m. and again just before midnight. - Retaliation was asked for and given, "A" & "B" Batteries firing 100 round each time. Howitzers are being kept rather short of ammunition these last few days.	
	6th.		Registration from new O.P. behind HINDENBURGH TRENCH. Aeroplane Target, transport moving, fired on by 3 Batteries at about 6.40.p.m. 72 rounds being fired. Night Firing :- "A" Battery fired 50 rounds per hour on the WONDER WORK and about the WELL.	

Army Form C. 2118

WAR DIARY
or
INTELLIGENCE SUMMARY
(Erase heading not required.)

Instructions regarding War Diaries and Intelligence Summaries are contained in F. S. Regs., Part II. and the Staff Manual respectively. Title Pages will be prepared in manuscript.

Place	Date	Hour	Summary of Events and Information	Remarks and references to Appendices
In the Field.	7th Sept.		One section of each Battery being relieved to night by the 58th Brigade R.F.A. 11th Division. No definite night firing ordered, but bursts of fire of 40 rounds at irregular intervals on new trenches shewn by Aeroplane photograph of to-day.	
	8th.		A barrage of 1 round per gun per 2 minutes kept up by the Brigade from 8.45. to 10.a.m. North of MOUQUET FARM from where the enemy made a bombing attack and put up a heavy barrage on our trenches. "B" Battery Wxxxxx by Hostile Shell. Lieut. Maurice Christie-Murray. The remaining section of each Battery and Brigade Headquarters are relieved at 8.p.m. and move to the wagon lines.	Wounded
	9th. & 10th.		General Routine at Wagon Lines - Lieut Maurice Christie Murray, died and is buried in the Military Cemetery, Rue de PERONNE, ALBERT.	
	11th		Reconnoitre for new positions in MASH VALLEY.	
	12th		Batteries are in action by 8.a.m. - Registration of trenches around THIEPVAL carried out during the day.	
	13th		Registration of targets for 25th Divisional Arty Operation Order No. 60. Building Gun pits etc., No night firing.	
	14th		Batteries check registers for to nights operation. Support 32nd Infantry Brigade 11th Division who attack at 6.30.p.m. as per 25th D.A. O.O. No.60. - Stop firing at 9.p.m. Enemy counter attack at midnight, all Batteries open fire which is kept up for 15 minutes.	
	15th		Last nights attack successful. - Enemy shell MASH VALLEY from 8.30. - 12 noon mostly with 7.7.c.m., Retaliate with 20 rounds per Battery, at 11.30.a.m. for hostile shelling of our trenches. - S.O.S. reported by 60th Bde. R.F.A. at 9.25.p.m. Open fire with all Batteries and fire 20 rounds per Battery and then 2 rounds per gun per minute for 10 minutes when firing is stopped.	

1875. Wt. W593/826 1,000,000 4/15 T.R.C. & A. A.D.S.S./Forms/C. 2118.

Army Form C. 2118

WAR DIARY
or
INTELLIGENCE SUMMARY

(Erase heading not required.)

Instructions regarding War Diaries and Intelligence Summaries are contained in F.S. Regs., Part II. and the Staff Manual respectively. Title Pages will be prepared in manuscript.

Place	Date	Hour	Summary of Events and Information	Remarks and references to Appendices
In the Field.	16th.		A few registers made by Batteries in the morning, "A", "C", & "D" (How) Bty, fired on aeroplane target at 12.50.p.m., 27 rounds were fired by each Battery. One other aeroplane target was engaged in the afternoon.	
	17th.		All Batteries fire on 2 Aeroplane Targets between 8.45. and 10.a.m. Three other Aeroplane targets engaged in the afternoon, 2 at extreme range were only engaged by "A" Battery. S.O.S. call for counter attack at 6.40. Brigade fires rapid rate for 10 minutes and ceases fire after 12 minutes. Brigade fires rapid rate for 10 Work carried out on Gun pits to enable guns to fire up to 8000 yards. Some registering done by Batteries.	
	18th.		All Batteries register JOSEPH'S TRENCH again. "A" Battery have 1 gun out of action. Very little shelling on both sides during the day. Enemy shell OVILLERS, MASH VALLEY, and POZIERES ROAD, LA BOISELLE, between 10.30.p.m. and 12.p.m. and at odd intervals during the night.	
	19th.		Batteries re-register targets for Divl. Arty. O.O. No. 61. Several Aeroplane targets received, but out of range. Hostile observation balloon reported by "B" Battery to have broken away and burst and to have fallen in the German Lines. Considerable activity of Aeroplanes throughout the day. There was a considerable amount of shelling fired at 9.45.p.m., 11.30.p.m., 2.a.m., and 3.45.a.m., from the direction of MOUQUET FARM and to the S.E. Quiet on our front.	
	20th.		At 12.15. enemy shelled our trenches with 7.7.c.m. and 42.c.m. for about 3 or 4 minutes. Daily allowance of Ammunition 18 pdr fired to-day as 166 rounds per Brigade. C/112 fired on a small party of Germans observed this afternoon and enemy result unknown. "A" Battery checked registers for barrages. New earthwork fired on. An instructional series fired by an "A" Btty Subalt: Other Batteries tested registers. MASH VALLEY was shelled at 9.15.p.m. with 10.5.c.m. and again between 1.a.m. and 2.a.m.	

Army Form C. 2118

WAR DIARY
or
INTELLIGENCE SUMMARY

(Erase heading not required.)

Instructions regarding War Diaries and Intelligence Summaries are contained in F. S. Regs., Part II. and the Staff Manual respectively. Title Pages will be prepared in manuscript.

Place	Date	Hour	Summary of Events and Information	Remarks and references to Appendices
In the Field.	21st.		MASH VALLEY was shelled at 9.10.a.m. with 10.5.c.m. Guns, Captain B. AURET Commanding "B" Battery, and 2nd Lieut. W.J. DUNLOP were killed. Shelling lifts onto ALBERT, LA BOISELLE ROAD at 9.55.a.m. Party of Germans in JOSEPH'S TRENCH fired on by "A" Battery. Several other parties fired on in the morning. HINDENBURG TRENCH shelled by 4.2" shell at 11.20 and 11.48.a.m. Eastern end of MASH VALLEY shelled continuously with 4.2" and 5.9" during the day. Two aeroplane targets - Guns in action - engaged in the evening. MASH VALLEY shelled at 7.30.p.m., 8.30.p.m., and about 9.30.p.m. with 4.2" & 7.7.c.m. An ammunition dump on the ALBERT, LA BOISELLE ROAD believed to be small arms, stokes bombs, etc, set on fire at 9.25.p.m. by hostile shell. MASH VALLEY and BAPAUME ROAD receive some attention during the night.	
	22nd.		Aeroplane target engaged at 9.a.m. 3 others engaged during the day. B.H.Q. move from MASH VALLEY to new position in an old communication trench about 400 yards in rear of old position. HINDENBURG TRENCH shelled between 6 and 7.p.m., also AVELUY about the same time with 4.2" and 5.9". MASH VALLEY shelled at about 7.30.p.m. "C" Battery two casualties at 7.50.p.m. 58th Brigade R.F.A. report "Enemy in possession of part of CONSTANCE TRENCH Batteries open fire at once. Counter attack being organised - Stop firing at 8.p.m. MASH VALLEY shelled intermittently during the night.	
	23rd.		Registrations carried out. O.P's reconnoitered in SKYLINE TRENCH. AVELUY Shelled about 10.30. and 11.p.m.	
	24th.		Work carried out by "A" Battery on new O.P. in SKYLINE TRENCH. Quiet morning. Some registration carried out by Batteries in afternoon. Enemy shell trenches in the vicinity of THEIPVAL between 4.45. and 5.p.m. One aeroplane target engaged.	
	25th.		Registration - Work on Gun Pits. Quiet on our front.	

WAR DIARY
or
INTELLIGENCE SUMMARY

(Erase heading not required.)

Army Form C. 2118

Place	Date	Hour	Summary of Events and Information	Remarks and references to Appendices
In the Field.	25th Continued.		Colonel checks Battery registers for Div. Arty O.O.'s 62 & 63. 3 Aeroplane targets engaged in afternoon. 2 Officers join :-	
	26th		Quiet in the morning. Support 18th Division who attack at 12.35.p.m. as per O.O. No. 62 & 63. "A" Battery was detailed to take on all aeroplane targets. 8 were engaged during the afternoon. Night firing carried out by all Batteries as ordered by D.H.Q. in front of our last objective. 50 rounds per hour from per Battery were fired. Hostile shelling and retaliation very feeble. 3430 rounds 18pdr and 720 rounds Hows: were fired in the afternoon.	
	27th		The Adjutant visits the captured trenches at THEIPVAL with 3 other Officers of the Brigade at dawn. Not one unexploded 18 pdr shell was noticed anywhere although thousands of shell cases were lying about. Hostile guns very quiet only an occasional round coming over. Enemy snipers and Machine Guns busy. Enemy shell SCHWABEN TRENCH and vicinity with 4.2" and 5.9" at about 11.15.a.m. 2 Aeroplane targets engaged by Batteries. Enemy shell THEIPVAL with 7.7.m.m. 7 Aeroplane targets engaged up to noon today. Another 3 Aeroplane targets engaged in the afternoon. Enemy shell West end of MASH VALLEY throughout the afternoon with 4.2" Lachramatory shell and a few 5.9" THEIPVAL was also very heavily shelled throughout the afternoon. Night firing same as last night.	
	28th		Aeroplane reported REGINA TRENCH full of Germans at 10.a.m. The Brigade fires 175 rounds in to it. Registrations carried out. Enemy shell N.E. outskirts of ALBERT about 11.30.a.m. Brigade supported 18th Division who continue attack on SCHWABEN REDOUBT at 1.p.m. as per 25th D.A. O.O. No. 65. Brigade and Battery Commanders reconnoitre for new positions in valley S.E. of THEIPVAL. Night firing by all Batteries carried out.	

Army Form C. 2118

WAR DIARY
or
INTELLIGENCE-SUMMARY

(Erase heading not required.)

Instructions regarding War Diaries and Intelligence Summaries are contained in F.S. Regs., Part II. and the Staff Manual respectively. Title Pages will be prepared in manuscript.

Place	Date	Hour	Summary of Events and Information	Remarks and references to Appendices
In the Field.	29th.		Brigade and Battery Commanders reconnoitre positions of 240th Brigade in the morning. Half battery reliefs carried out in accordance with 25th D.A. O.O. 66. Enemy counter attack on our left, Part of SCHWABEN REDOUBT captured. Brigade opens fire and fires 2 rounds per gun per minute. Enemy shelling very continous throughout the day. Enemy attacked STUFF REDOUBT, Brigade opens S.O.S. sent up in the evening. Enemy attacked STUFF REDOUBT, Brigade opens fire. Night firing carried out by the Brigade as last night.	
	30th		Enemy attack SCHWABEN REDOUBT in the early hours of the morning. Brigade Commander reconnoitres O.P's and gun positions of new MERK area. Support attack of 18th Division who attack SCHWABEN REDOUBT at 4 p.m. as per 25th DivL Arty O.O. 67. Relief of 2nd and half Battery carried out this evening. Our Brigade Front is taken over by 84th Brigade, R.F.A.	

Lieut. Col. R.F.A.
Commanding 112th Brigade R.F.A.

25th. DIVISIONAL ARTILLERY

112th. BRIGADE R. F. A.

25th. DIVISIONAL ARTILLERY

OCTOBER 1916.

Army Form C. 2118.

112 Bde RFA
Vol XIV

Vol 12

WAR DIARY
or
INTELLIGENCE SUMMARY
(Erase heading not required.)

Place	Date	Hour	Summary of Events and Information	Remarks and references to Appendices
In the field	Oct 1st		Brigade Headquarters move to new position behind USNA Redoubt. — Take over from RA Group 48th Div. at 9 a.m. — We are now supporting our own Infantry. — Colonel reconnoitres OP's and new Battery positions with Battery Commanders. — Night firing 35 rounds per hour.	
	2nd		Registration of Targets for Div Arty. O.O. 68 — work on OP's and dug-outs etc. — Mash Valley was shelled several times during day — Operation postponed on account of weather. — work on Gun pits — some night firing attempted.	
	3rd		Counter attack manages checked from front line. Registration checked and work on gun pit dugouts. Night firing 25 rounds per hour.	
	4th		Some work on gun pits carried out — Check registers — Quiet on our front. — Persistant shelling with 5.9 and 4.2 around Battery positions around POZIERES from Noon to 6 p.m. Battery approaches to ALBERT and BAPAUME Rd Shelled at 1.15 a.m. and 2.15 a.m. — B. Battery move to new position. A. Battery move one Section to new position in POZIERES. Night firing 25 rounds per hour.	

Army Form C. 2118.

112 Bde RFA
Vol XIV

WAR DIARY
or
INTELLIGENCE SUMMARY

(Erase heading not required.)

Instructions regarding War Diaries and Intelligence Summaries are contained in F.S. Regs., Part II. and the Staff Manual respectively. Title Pages will be prepared in manuscript.

Place	Date	Hour	Summary of Events and Information	Remarks and references to Appendices
In The Field	5th Oct 1916		Registration by A + B Batteries - C Battery start wire cutting but are stopped by order of Div Arty. - BAPAUME Road shelled close to POZIERES at 1 pm - Battery firing intermittently throughout the day - About 20 rounds fired around Western end of MASH VALLEY at 10.7 pm	
	6th		On target registered by C Battery with Aeroplane observation Work on New OPs by POZIERES Windmill - Night firing 35 rds per hour for Gun 18 per Battery and 15 rounds per hour per How.	
	7th		Fired in accordance with orders received from Div Arty. - SOS reported about 6.30 pm Brigade put on our front - opened out with rapid fire for 10 minutes - A false alarm. Vicinity of POZIERES shelled during afternoon and evening	
	8th		Support Canadian who attack at 4.50 am as per Div Arty. OO 69. - Night firing 25 rds per how and trench of fire by Brigade at 5.6.7 am - 4 rounds per gun fired each time	

112 Bde RFA Army Form C. 2118.
Vol XIV

WAR DIARY
or
INTELLIGENCE SUMMARY
(Erase heading not required.)

Instructions regarding War Diaries and Intelligence Summaries are contained in F.S. Regs., Part II. and the Staff Manual respectively. Title Pages will be prepared in manuscript.

Place	Date	Hour	Summary of Events and Information	Remarks and references to Appendices
In the field	9th Oct 1916	12.35 p.m.	Support w/s Inf Bde who attacked as per 25th D.A. O.O. 70 at 12.35 p.m. – Germans attack N.E. of Stuff Redoubt about 6 p.m. – Brigade open out with rapid fire. S.O.S. reported on both flanks of our line – Brigade opens out fire which is stopped after 10 minutes.	
	10th		Nothing unusual to report. – Quiet. – Night firing as usual.	
	11th		Nothing unusual to report. – Quiet in morning. – S.O.S. reported Stuff Redoubt about 3 p.m. – Brigade fire for about ½ hour. No attack is made	
	12th		Some Enemy Shelling about R 27 d with 10.5 cm. – Rate 1 round per minute from MIRAMONT. – Commences 2.20 pm. Ceases 2.45 pm at 3 pm MASH Valley shelled with 4.2. – Our guns turned S.O.S. Stuff Redoubt at about 2.30 pm. – All guns turned on us at 4. – 4.30 pm and 9 pm.	
	13th		Quiet in morning. – Enemy Heavy Battery firstime around POZIERES.	

2449 Wt. W14957/M90 750,000 1/16 J.B.C. & A. Forms/C.2118/12.

112 Bde RFA
Vol XIV

Army Form C. 2118

WAR DIARY
or
INTELLIGENCE SUMMARY
(Erase heading not required.)

Instructions regarding War Diaries and Intelligence Summaries are contained in F.S. Regs., Part II. and the Staff Manual respectively. Title Pages will be prepared in manuscript.

Place	Date	Hour	Summary of Events and Information	Remarks and references to Appendices
In The Field	14th Oct 1916		Hostile shelling normal except on communication trenches in our zone. Support 1st Inf. Bde who attack at 2.41 pm as per O.O II — Slight firing 150 rounds 18 pdr and 50 rounds 4.5 How per Bde during the night.	
	15th		Situation normal — Hostile Artillery very quiet — Slight machine Gun fire in front of P19 — 15 to the left — 12 Bn commanders observation Trenches reported on GRAND COURT — MIRAMONT road — "A" Battery fired occasional bursts on it during the day.	
	16th		Quiet on our front — Colonel Butler leaves the Brigade to join Overseas Gunnery school at Salisbury Plain — Colonel A.D.S. Johnson D.S.O. joins the Brigade — during night firing 350 rounds 18 pdr and 60 rounds 4.5" Hows: — during night MASH Valley shelled during night with lachrymatory and gas shell.	
	17th & 18th		All 18 pdrs wire cutting	
	19th		Enemy keep up a heavy barrage all along the front throughout the day. Several S.O.S. Signals reported off our zone — Wire kept under fire day and night	

112 Bde RFA
Vol XIV

Army Form C. 2118

WAR DIARY
or
INTELLIGENCE SUMMARY
(Erase heading not required.)

Instructions regarding War Diaries and Intelligence Summaries are contained in F.S. Regs., Part II. and the Staff Manual respectively. Title Pages will be prepared in manuscript.

Place	Date	Hour	Summary of Events and Information	Remarks and references to Appendices
In the Field	26th Oct 1916		Enemy shelled our front line at about 5.30 am North of SCHWABEN. Our OP has his occasionally at the wire – night firing as ordered in B.M. 644. – Nothing abnormal happened at our front during the night	
	21st		Batteries continued firing occasionally at the wire – 12-6 pm 25th Divl Inf attack and take REGINA Trench as per O.O. 72 – Our Batteries fired according to programme. – 5 aeroplane targets engaged during operations – Night firing on wire in front of GRANDCOURT Trench and NEW Trench.	
	22nd		All 18 pdr Batteries cut wire at GRANDCOURT Trench – Hostile artillery quiet – Night firing as last night	
	23rd		All Batteries fire with one Section from 6 am – 6.15 am as per instructions from Div Arty Hdqn for intense bombardment. "D" Battery move to new position close to "B" Battery on SKYLINE Trench. – Night firing as ordered in B.M. 677. D Batterys move completed. – No heavy enemy firing reported.	
	24th		6 18 pdrs and 2 Hows bombarded GRANDCOURT Trench – SOUTH MIRAMOUNT Trench as per orders from Div Arty. – Wire cutting continued also preparation of new positions – Night firing as instructed by Div Arty. – No abnormal enemy fire reported.	

112 Bde RFA
Vol XIV

Army Form C. 2118

Instructions regarding War Diaries and Intelligence Summaries are contained in F.S. Regs., Part II. and the Staff Manual respectively. Title Pages will be prepared in manuscript.

WAR DIARY
or
INTELLIGENCE SUMMARY
(Erase heading not required.)

Place	Date	Hour	Summary of Events and Information	Remarks and references to Appendices
In the field	25th Oct 1916		Wire cutting still in progress by 18 pdrs. - Several aeroplane targets engaged. - Moves of B & D cancelled owing to weather conditions. Obtained rounds during day into 16 o 05' - 74 - Night firing as ordered by Div Arty.	
	26th		At 5 a.m. enemy started firing heavily on THIEPVAL Area - SCHWABEN STUFF and ZOLLERN redoubts. - Our batteries retaliated - Bombardment of GRANDCOURT & S. MIRAMONT. Trenches as per instructions from DIV. ARTY. - Wire cutting still continued. B moves all its guns to new position at R.23.d.1.3 and D into hours 29.6.48. - Night firing as ordered.	
	27th		Bombardment started again as in morning of 26th - Wire cutting continued by A & C. B reports all guns in new position. D - shot one line in and one on stock of German trenches damaged. Our front during afternoon.	
	28th		No unusual enemy activity - B Battery continued to carry on their ammunition. B.H.Q. moved to new position in R.32.c.4.0 Night firing carried out by A & C. - B & D spend night in carrying over ammunition to new positions.	
	29th		Nothing unusual to report - wire cutting continued by A & C. R.S.S., B & D working on new positions and getting up ammunition.	

1875 Wt. W593/826 1,000,000 4/15 J.B.C. & A. A.D.S.S./Forms/C.2118.

112 Bde RFA
Vol XIV Army Form C. 2118

WAR DIARY
or
INTELLIGENCE SUMMARY
(Erase heading not required.)

Place	Date	Hour	Summary of Events and Information	Remarks and references to Appendices
In The Field	30th Oct 1916		No visibility - little firing carried out - Some hostile shelling on BAPAUME Road and shrunk ZOLLERN Trench - Two 18 pdr out of action 1. buffer trouble, other condemned for serving - 150 rounds fired during night.	
	31st		Hostile shelling in morning very numerous N of POZIERES - MASH VALLEY - OVILLERS - WOLGEN Lists E of Road ANCRE and ALBERT road receiving a little attention	

[signature]
Lt. Col. R.F.A.
Comd'g 112th Brigade R.F.A.

112th. BRIGADE R. F. A.

25th. DIVISIONAL ARTILLERY

N O V E M B E R 1 9 1 6.

WAR DIARY or INTELLIGENCE SUMMARY

(Erase heading not required.)

112th Brigade R.F.A. Army Form C. 2118
November 1916
Vol 45

Place	Date	Hour	Summary of Events and Information	Remarks and references to Appendices
In The Field Sheet 57D S.E. R.33.d.2.5.	1st Nov., 1916.		Wire Cutting carried out by two 18 pdr Batteries of the Brigade during the day.	
	2nd.		Wire Cutting continued - Night Firing by "A" & "C" Batteries - "D" Battery brought up their ammunition at the guns to full compliment. - Enemy shelled POZIERES and to the W of it with heavy shells during the afternoon and evening.	
	3rd.		Wire Cutting continued - Brigade Look-out reported having seen a gun firing from E of DOVECOTE and also much traffic seen on road through G.26 - 27.	
	4th.		Wire Cutting continued - Brigade Look-out reported shelling about COURCELETTE and a light barrage along the whole front at 4.45 lasting about 2 minutes. - Night firing 150 rounds fired by the Brigade to prevent work on new Trenches.	
	5th.		Wire Cutting still being continued by the Brigade - Heavy firing reported north of SCHWABEN by the Brigade Look-out about 9.15.	
	6th.		Wire cutting continued by 18 pdrs - No abnormal enemy Artillery activivity reported. Night firing 150 rounds by the Brigade to prevent work by enemy on trenches and wire.	
	7th.		Wire cutting continued - "A" Battery altered their position to enable them to shoot at new target. Night firing 75v rounds each by "A" & "C" on paths and trenches in the Brigade Zone	
	8th.		Nothing abnormal to report - "A" & "C" Batteries carried out the usual morning bombardment from 5.45 to 6.a.m. - Wire cutting continued by 18 prds - No undue enemy artillery activity reported. Night firing 150 rounds by "C" Battery on to wire and trenches in Brigade area to prevent enemy work.	
	9th.		Wire cutting still being carried on. - "D" Battery reported that they were being shelled by 4.2" from the direction of LOPART WOOD - 4 rounds per minute. - The enemy shelled all night around R.33.c. & d. with gas shells - "C" Battery had a gun put out of action by enemy shell.	

Army Form C. 2118

112th Brigade RFA
November 1915
Vol /5

WAR DIARY
or
INTELLIGENCE SUMMARY
(Erase heading not required.)

Instructions regarding War Diaries and Intelligence Summaries are contained in F.S. Regs., Part II. and the Staff Manual respectively. Title Pages will be prepared in manuscript.

Place	Date	Hour	Summary of Events and Information	Remarks and references to Appendices
In the Field.	10th		18 pdrs continue wire cutting – "D" Battery had one How: destroyed by enemy fire. Enemy continued bombarding with gas shell until 6.a.m. – From 5.30. to 6.a.m. a bombardment of GRANDCOURT Trench and S. MIRAMOUNT Trench was carried out.	
Sheet 57DSE R 33 d 9.5	11th		Wire cutting continued – "A" Battery have to alter their position to be able to shoot at R.15.c.O.-45 – R.14.d.6510. according to B.M./823. Brigade has now 3 guns out of action one each from "C" & "D" Batteries destroyed by enemy shell fire and one of "A" Battery's with spring trouble.	
	12th		Wire cutting continued and final preparations made for carrying out O.O. 75 – There was the usual morning bombardment at 5.45.a.m. and in addition to night firing bombardments were carried out at 11 and 11.30.	
	13th		Brigade supported the attack of 19th Division at 5.45.a.m. as per 25th D.A. O.O. 75. Considerable enemy fire was reported at different times during the evening. 150 rounds fired during night by "A" Battery as ordered by Div. Arty.	
	14th		At 6.30. a heavy bombardment started in our left by our own guns. Reports of enemy fire kept coming in and were reported to Division. "D" & "C" Batteries are firing occasional rounds on to the same targets as yesterday. "A" Battery also fire occasional rounds at the wire in front of GRANDCOURT Trench and DESIRE Trench.	
	15th		"A" & "C" Batteries cut wire in front of DESIRE Trench – "D" Battery fired 33 rounds on DESIRE Trench – Night firing carried out by "A" Battery who fired 150 rounds on DESIRE and GRANDCOURT Trenches.	
	16th		"A" & "C" Batteries did observed shooting on the wire in front of DESIRE Trench and "D" Battery fired a few rounds observed fire at DESIRE Trench itself.	
	17th		Wire Cutting by "A" & "CW Batteries in front of DESIRE Trench continues – Each Battery firing 500 rounds during the day – "D" Battery fire 33 rounds at the same trench. Night firing "A" Battery fired 150 rounds on to Desire Trench.	

112th Brigade Army Form C. 2118
R.F.A.
November 1916
VOL 15

WAR DIARY
or
INTELLIGENCE SUMMARY
(Erase heading not required.)

Place	Date	Hour	Summary of Events and Information	Remarks and references to Appendices
In the Field	18th		Attack successfully carried out by 4th Canadians, 18th & 19th Divisions on DESIRE Trench and to outskirts of GRANDCOURT - Night firing on communications behind GRANDCOURT Trench 150 rounds during the night.	
Shab 57D SE R.33 d.25	19th		Slight and promiscuous hostile shelling during the morning - At about 4.10.p.m. the enemy were reported to be massing in GRANDCOURT Trench - All the 112th Brigade Batteries opened fire at 2 rounds per gun per minute until ordered to stop by the Division - Night firing carried out by "C" Battery who fired 150 rounds during the night.	
	20th		NOTHING to report.	
	21st		B.H.Q. and Batteries move to Wagon Lines - Front being covered until 12 noon - Ammunition handed over at the Gun positions.	
	22nd.		Preparing for March - Corps Commander inspects the Division in the afternoon and bids us farewell.	
	23rd		Brigade leaves camp at 9.a.m. and marches to AMPLIER and billets for the night.	
	24th		Brigade marches from AMPLIER TO CONCHY-sur-CANCHE and billets for the night.	
	25th		Brigade marches from CONCHY-sur-CANCHE to HESTRUS and billets.	
	26th		Brigade at HESTRUS - General cleaning up and arranging for re-organisation of the Brigade to 6 gun 18 pdr Batteries.	
	27th		Brigade still at HESTRUS - General duties being carried out.	
	28th		Brigade marched to WESTRNHEM and billeted for the night.	
	29th		Brigade marched to BOSEGHEM and billeted for the night.	
	30th		Brigade left BOSEGHEM and marched to METEREN and billetted there.	

Lieut. Col. R.F.A.
Commanding 112th Brigade R.F.A.

25th. DIVISIONAL ARTILLERY

112th. BRIGADE R. F. A.

25th. DIVISIONAL ARTILLERY

DECEMBER 1916.

Army Form C. 2118

112 Bde RFA

Vol December page 1

WAR DIARY
or
INTELLIGENCE-SUMMARY
(Erase heading not required.)

Instructions regarding War Diaries and Intelligence Summaries are contained in F. S. Regs., Part II. and the Staff Manual respectively. Title Pages will be prepared in manuscript.

Place	Date	Hour	Summary of Events and Information	Remarks and references to Appendices
In The Field.	December 1st, 1916.		Brigade at METEREN - General duties being carried out.	
	2nd.		Brigade still at METEREN - General duties being carried out.	
	3rd.		Brigade at METEREN.	
	4th.		Brigade move forward and took over the front.	
	5th.		Visibility was poor throughout the day. Enemy Artillery fire was not very active. About 50 rounds of 7.7. wre fired at 2 minutes interval starting at 12.30.p.m. on to U.25.c.8.6½. Intermittent rifle grenades apparently from Factory Farm throughout the day. A gas alarm at midnight but no gas experienced.	
	6th.		Rifle Grenades were fired by the enemy about U.15.d.5.3. throughout the day. Our T.M's retaliated between 3. and 3.30.p.m. - Enemy Artillery quiet.	
	7th.		Very bad visibilty 10.30. to 11.45.a.m. Left Sub Group co-operated with Heavy T.M's. Enemy retaliation practically negligable, G.O.C. R.A. lXth Corps visited batteries of this Brigade.	
	8th.		Visibilty again very bad. - No Artillery activity and just a few T.M's and rifle grenades throughout the day - B.G. R.A. Visited Wagon Lines.	
	9th.		Another quiet day - A little enemy movement observed about 9.40.a.m.	
	10th.		New timber reported to be added to dump in U.22½c.60.7½.. At 3.15 two parties of 3 men each were seen moving about this point - Otherwise nothing to report.	
	11th.		New work done on enemy's front line at U.16.c.0.0. No enemy fire of any kind reported.	
	12th.		Nothing of interest to report.	

Army Form C. 2118

WAR DIARY
or
INTELLIGENCE SUMMARY
(Erase heading not required.)

Place	Date	Hour	Summary of Events and Information	Remarks and references to Appendices
In the Field.	13th Dec. 1916.		At 10.30.a.m. two men were seen working at U.22.c.75.75. for 5 minutes. Enemy Artillery and T.M's were not active.	
	14th		A party of about 30 men were seen working in a trench but were dispersed by "A" Battery about 10.35.a.m. - Otherwise nothing to report.	
	15th		Two wire cutting shoots carried out from 9.30. to 10.a.m. and 3.15. to 3.45.p.m. by 2" T.M's The enemy retaliated with varied effect - With T.M's and Artillery - RUTTERS LODGE received some attention from 4.2". - Our own fire was reported to be effective. B/112, B/110, and D/112. each fired 50 rounds on each occasion to cover the T.M's.	
	16th		General Bainbridge visited the Batteries of the group in the morning - No activity of any kind.	
	17th		Left Sub group stood by in support of M.G's and Stokes mortars from 5.30.a.m. to 6.30.a.m. Hostile T.M's 9 and 12 were engaged who tried to retaliate.	
	18th		G.O.C. 2nd Army inspected the batteries of the group. Observation was impossible most of the morning owing to the mist. At 1.p.m. our T.M's shelled enemy's Line S. of BROKEN TREE FARM At 1.40. enemy shelled the road in U.14.a. &c. - Otherwise no enemy fire to report.	
	19th.		NOTHING TO REPORT.	
	20th.		The Commander-in-Chief inspected a detachment of 5 men and 1 Officer from each Battery at ROMARIN. From 3.10.p.m. to 3.40.p.m. wire cutting was carried out by 2" T.M's which was reported to be very effective. Enemy retaliated with T.M's and also a 4.2" fired about 15 rounds starting at 3.40.p.m. into RUTTER LODGE.	
	21st.		Very little Artillery fire during day. - A party of Germans were seen on road leading to WARNETON and fired at with apparently good effect. T.M's were very active.	
	22nd.		Enemy shell with 4.2" Hows: the vicinities of HYDE PARK CORNER and RUTTER LODGE. T.M's very active around LA GHEER - Small bombardment of enemy's trenches at 8.a.m. by 2 6 gun Batteries - about 100 rounds being fired.	

112 Brigade RFA
Army Form C. 2118

December page 3

WAR DIARY
or
INTELLIGENCE-SUMMARY
(Erase heading not required.)

Instructions regarding War Diaries and Intelligence Summaries are contained in F.S. Regs., Part II. and the Staff Manual respectively. Title Pages will be prepared in manuscript.

Place	Date	Hour	Summary of Events and Information	Remarks and references to Appendices
In the Field.	23rd DEC. 1916.		T.M's cut wire for raid as per 25th Div. Arty Order No. 91. Hostile T.M's active throughout the day, Except for light retaliation our Artillery was quiet throughout the day - A small barrage was put on the German Front Line at 9.p.m.	
	24th.		Hostile T.M's very active. - Retaliation was given by 2 salves from 4.5" Hows: on each T.M. when it opened fire - Hostile Artillery fairly active. - Our T.M's continued Wire cutting to-day.	
	25th.		Except for some T.M. Fire about 7.a.m. the enemy were exceptionally quiet on our front throughout the day. The 11th Battalion Cheshire Regt raid the enemy's trenches at 9.p.m. as per 25th Divl Arty order No. 91. This group of Artillery fired foe 35 minutes - 1600 18 pdr H.E. and 300 B.X. being expended in that time. - Retaliation by the enemy very feeble - Hostile Artillery very slow about opening fire.	
	26th.		Infantry very satisfied with lasts nights barrage - Visibility very poor - Artillery quiet on both sides.	
	27th.		Artillery fairly active on both sides - Nothing unusual to report - Visibility poor.	
	28th.		Hostile fire about normal - "B" Battery 112th Brigade R.F.A. and vicinity was shelled during the morning with about 100 10.c.m. shell. The Colonel Commanding gives a lecture un Gunnery at METEREN.	
	29th.		Co-operate in wire cutting operation from 2.p.m. to 2.30.p. - Covering fire was put on Enemy's T.M.'s and trenches - 300 rounds 18 pdr and 210 rounds How: ammunition being expended. Hostile retaliation very feeble.	
	30th.		Brigade Headquarters moves to Hutments on the PLOEGSTEERT and ROMARIN Road. Lieut. Col. Forman, D.S.O. preceeds on leave. - Lieut. Col. Lambarde, D.S.O. assumes command.	
	31st.		Very quiet day. - Batteries registered for the wire cutting operation to be carried out on the 1st Jan 1917.	

Commanding 112th Brigade R.F.A.

Page 1.

Army Form C. 2118

WAR DIARY or INTELLIGENCE SUMMARY

January, 1917. 112th Brigade, R.F.A. Volume XVII.

(Erase heading not required.)

J.M/15

Place	Date	Hour	Summary of Events and Information	Remarks and references to Appendices
In the Field.	1st Jany 1917.		Wire Cutting operation at 10.30.a.m. to 11.15 a.m. as per 25th Divl Arty Order. Enemy's T.M's were silenced when they retaliated. - Hostile retaliation very weak.	
	2nd.		Hostile Shelling more active than usual in and around PLOEGSTEERT Wood.	
	3rd.		Little Artillery fire - Some movement seen at TILLET FARM and fired on.	
	4th.		No undue Artillery activity reported - A German Balloon seen from RUTTERS LODGE ascended for 8 minutes just before 2.p.m.	
	5th.		G.O.C./2nd Army visited the batteries. Visibility good - A working party reported cleaning trench at U.16.b.7.5. at 2.50.p.m. - about 50 high air bursts into T.17.d. between 2.p.m. & 4.p.m. R.A.	
	6th.		Visibility low - No enemy Artillery fire of any kind reported - A very quiet day.	
	7th.		Nothing to report.	
	8th.		Both sides were again ver quiet.	
	9th.		A wire cutting and destructive operation was carried out by our T.M's and Artillery on U.15 & 16.	
	10th.		Nothing to report. - One of our observation balloons seen to fall in flames near DRANOUTRE, brought down by hostile aircraft.	
	11th.		Nothing reported - Visibility bad and weather snowy.	
	12th.		Enemy Artillery slightly more active over 100 rounds 4.2" how fell in the area during day. a party of 15 men dispersed at 10.15.a.m. by "C" Battery at U.16.b.9.8.	
	13th.		Heavy rain and sleet all day nothing to report.	

Page 2.
Army Form C. 2118

WAR DIARY
or
INTELLIGENCE SUMMARY

January 1917. /12th Brigade RFA

(Erase heading not required.)

Instructions regarding War Diaries and Intelligence Summaries are contained in F.S. Regs., Part II. and the Staff Manual respectively. Title Pages will be prepared in manuscript.

Place	Date	Hour	Summary of Events and Information	Remarks and references to Appendices
In the Field.	Jany 14th 1917.		Thick mist prevented good observation on both sides - Both sides were active.	
	15th.		The Same conditions as yesterday.	
	16th.		A quiet day with bad conditions.	
	17th.		Nothing to report except that a working party at U.22.a.4.6. was dispersed by our fire at 3.50.p.m.	
	18th.		Bombardment of enemy front line and support carried out from 2.5.p.m. to 3.20.p.m. just South of LE GHEER ROAD. - Enemy retaliation not excessive though a 5.9" did some good shooting on LOWNDES AVENUE.	
	19th.		Enemy Artillery and T.M's active about U.15. central and D.& C and D Batteries retaliated. Hostile Artillery slightly more active than usual.	
	20th.		Enemy Artillery and T.M's were again active on our front. No's 9., 10., 11., 12., 14., 15., 16., and 17 were all active during the day and were retaliated on with good effect.	
	21st.		G.O.C. 25th Division visited the Brigade Wagon Lines during the morning.	
	22nd.		The morning was quiet but at 1.55.p.m. enemy started a heavy bombardment with T.M's of all calibre on the whole of our front, especially on the two northern most zones. This was kept up till 8.p.m. and we retaliated hard all the time. The Germans entered our lines at AUTON FARM; U.15.1. and opposite RUTTERS LODGE.	
	23rd.		Very quiet day.- Enemy aircraft were very active during the day.	
	24th.		Colonel Forman, D.S.O. rejoined the Brigade from the Division.- Enemy aircraft active, but nothing else to report.	

Page 3

Army Form C. 2118

WAR DIARY
or
INTELLIGENCE SUMMARY
(Erase heading not required.)

January 1917. 112th Brigade RFA.

Instructions regarding War Diaries and Intelligence Summaries are contained in F.S. Regs., Part II. and the Staff Manual respectively. Title Pages will be prepared in manuscript.

Place	Date	Hour	Summary of Events and Information	Remarks and references to Appendices
In the Field.	25th Jany 1917.		2nd. Lieut. Kay and 2nd Lieut Jounson were posted to C. & A. Batteries respectively. At 2.p.m. B/112 fired about 100 rounds at enemy front line in the vicinity of U.22.c.2½.7. to cover T.M's wire cutting at that point. Enemy fired about 200 4.2" and 5.9" during the early forenoon xx on T.17. - Aircraft on both sides very active.	
	26th.		Enemy aircraft very active indeed all day. They observed all the morning while the enemy put about 400 4.2" into T.17, but no damage was reported from this.	
	27th.		Enemy aircraft very active - "B" Battery covered T.M's wire cutting at U.22.a.3½.7. between 3 and 3.30.p.m. - Enemy Artillery in-active.	
	28th.		"C" Battery supported small wire cutting operation in conjunction with T.M's and Stokes in U.15.a. - Enemy aircraft very active.	
	29th.		"A" Battery supported another small wire cutting shoot at U.22.a.2½.½. - Aircraft again active on both sides - "A" Battery tested an enfilade gun at C.1.d.4.5½. with satisfactory results.	
	30th.		From 10.a.m. to 11.a.m. enemy registered our front line in U.21.b. and also NEW CUT (U.21.b.2.3.) with about 40 rounds 7.7.mm. from DEULEMONT - Large percentage blinds.	
	31st.		"B" Battery assisted in minor wire cutting operation at U.22.a.0.2½. firing about 100 rounds Hostile aircraft much less active but ours very active during the afternoon - From 4 to 6.p.m. enemy shelled intermittently T.17.d. with 5.9"s	

[signature]
Lieut. Col. R.F.A.
Commanding 112th Brigade R.F.A.

Page 1.
Army Form C. 2118

Vol 16
Volume XVIII

112th Brigade W.D.

WAR DIARY
or
INTELLIGENCE SUMMARY
(Erase heading not required.)

February 1917

Instructions regarding War Diaries and Intelligence Summaries are contained in F.S. Regs., Part II. and the Staff Manual respectively. Title Pages will be prepared in manuscript.

Place	Date	Hour	Summary of Events and Information	Remarks and references to Appendices
In The Field	Febry 1st 1917		The enemy aircraft was very active crossing our line on many occasions. About 5.30.a.m. T.24.d. & T.18.d. were shelled by 4.2". About 5.5. an S.O.S. was reported from Right Group and also a fake alarm came from our Right Battalion.	
	2nd.		Aeroplanes of both sides were very active. Both Artilleries were quiet all day except at 9.a.m. enemy appeared to be registering our Front Line in U.21.a. - dropping 2 in his own trenches.	
	3rd.		Visibility poor all day. - A German aeroplane dropped a message about 2 of our airmen near "C" Battery - From 2.15. to 3.45 enemy intermittently shelled LONE HOUSE area with 5.9"s	
	4th.		Visibility poor again - George and Christopher reported active between 3.30. to 4.45.p.m. and were silenced by our Hows:	
	5th.		We carried out a destructive and wire cutting bombardment in U.15.b. from 2.30. to 3.30.p.m. Enemy retaliation negligable - Visibility very poor - Enemy aircraft fairly active.	
	6th.		Visibility poor all day and both sides were quiet - about 4.p.m. 20 rounds 4.2" were fired by enemy on Front line in U.28.a. and U.22.c.	
	7th		Fairly quiet day - About 25 7.7mm. fell in U.21.b. and 30 4.2" in U.8.c. - Both Batteries seemed to be in the direction of WARNETON. - Hostile aircraft very active. - Parties of 1, 2, and 3 men respectively seen and fired on, on light railway about U.3.c.8.5. - Visibility very fair.	
	8th.		Our T.M's were fairly active but only 7 rounds of enemy fire were reported during the entire day. - Aircraft of both sides active. - A little movement was observed behind the lines and visibility was good.	
	9th.		Enemy Artillery were active up till about 2.p.m. numerous points being shelled - "A" Battery (U.15.a.) were registered with 5.9" and 4.2" with aeroplane observation between 1.15. and 2.15.p.m. - Visibility was very good and aircraft were active. Several parties were observed behind enemy line and were fired.	

1875 Wt. W593/826 1,000,000 4/15 J.B.C. & A. A.D.S.S./Forms/C. 2118.

Page 2

Army Form C. 2118

WAR DIARY
or
INTELLIGENCE SUMMARY
(Erase heading not required.)

112th Brigade R.F.A.

Instructions regarding War Diaries and Intelligence Summaries are contained in F. S. Regs., Part II. and the Staff Manual respectively. Title Pages will be prepared in manuscript.

Place	Date	Hour	Summary of Events and Information	Remarks and references to Appendices
In the Field.	Feb 10th 1917		From 7.30. to 11.a.m. "G" Batteries detached section was registered and heavily shelled with 5.9's (300) One gun destroyed. - Aeroplane observed most of the time.	
	11th		2nd Lieut A.B. Laxton joined the Brigade and was posted to "G" Battery - Quiet day - George fired 5 rounds, but was at once retaliated on and silenced. - Enemy Artillery was not active. - Aircraft less active.	
	12th		Visibility bad and no aircraft activity. - Gilbert George and Christopher were active at different times during the day but were silenced at once with accurate fire.	
	13th		Aircraft on both sides were active. - Artillery and T.M's were quiet.	
	14th		The 150th Brigade R.F.A. and and Army Brigade composed of B/77, C/77, C/180, and B/173, came into action and were attached to us.	
	15th		Attached Batteries started registering - A bombardment and wire cutting on German support and front line in U.15.a. carried out between 12.30. and 1.30.p.m. - 1200 18 pdr and 400 How shells fired.	
	16th		Attached Batteries finished registering - Nothing else to report.	
	17th		C/173 and D/113 attached to the Brigade for the raid. - At 10.40.a.m. the 1st Wilts and the 10th Cheshires raided the trenches N. & S. of FACTORY FARM. - The attached batteries moved out after dark.	
	18th		The 8th S.L. made a raid at 11.p.m. on the right sector and A and D Batteries co-operated under orders from Right Group. - "A" Battery fired 800 rounds and "D" Battery 400 rounds.	
	19th		Very bad visibility and a quiet day. - "D" Battery fired 93 rounds on a T.M. firing from about U.15.a.97.95.	
	20th		Visibility was again poor and no activity was reported except that a few T.M.s which were at once retaliated on	

Page 3

Army Form C. 2118

WAR DIARY
or
INTELLIGENCE-SUMMARY
(Erase heading not required.)

112th Brigade R.F.A.

Instructions regarding War Diaries and Intelligence Summaries are contained in F.S. Regs., Part II. and the Staff Manual respectively. Title Pages will be prepared in manuscript.

Place	Date	Hour	Summary of Events and Information	Remarks and references to Appendices
In the Field	Feby 21st 1917		A raid was carried out by 36th Division in the evening :- "A" Battery fired 540 rounds - "G" Battery fired 540 rounds - "D" Battery fired 240 rounds . Quiet day except for a few T.M's about ST YVES and RUTTERS LODGE - Visibility very poor.	
	22nd		Quiet day - Visibility very poor - T.M's inactive.	
	23rd.		4. T.M's were reported to fall in U.15.c. from BLACK SHED - At 6.a.m. the enemy's T.M's very active - attempted raid by the enemy - "A" Battery fired 19 rds "G" Battery fired 67 rds "D" Battery fired 18 rds on T.M's in retaliation - Visibility bad.	
	24th.		Very quiet on our front all day - At 10.a.m. heavy firing much further on our part was heard South of our Sector.	
	25th.		Christopher and George was active at 4.15., but were retaliated on and stopped by our 4.5" Between 200 and 300 rounds of 4.2" and 5.9" some of which were gas were fired into T.17. None of these fell near any battery.	
	26th.		Visibility was good, but the day was exceptionally quiet. No enemy Artillery or T.M. Fire at all was reported, and our Artillery was quiet. One section of each Battery was relieved by the N.Z.A.	
	27th.		Very quiet day. - Remaining sections of Batteries were relieved and proceeded to their respective Wagon Lines.	
	28th		Batteries and Brigade Headquarters at respective Wagon Lines - General Cleaning and packing up ready for the move to Rest Area.	

[signature]
Lieut. Col. R.A.
Commanding 112th Brigade R.F.A.

March 1917

Army Form C. 2118.

112TH Brigade R.F.A

WAR DIARY
or
INTELLIGENCE SUMMARY.
(Erase heading not required.)

Place	Date	Hour	Summary of Events and Information	Remarks and references to Appendices
In The Field	1/3/17	—	Brigade marched from wagon lines to EBBINGHEM arriving about 4 p.m. – Fine day – 90B & C RA dispersed Brigade on the BAILLEUL. Rd	
	2/3/17	9am	Brigade marched from EBBINGHEM to ESQUERDES arriving 12.30 pm – Fine day.	
	3/3/17		General cleaning up and disinfecting of stables in ESQUERDES	
	4/3/17		Kit inspections and general duties during morning – Football Matches in the afternoon	
	5/3/17		Section Drill order and gun drills in Batteries – Harness cleaning etc in afternoon – The Brigade Signal Officer started training 32 O.R Signallers from the Brigade.	

Page 2

March 1917

112th Brigade R.F.A.

WAR DIARY
or
INTELLIGENCE SUMMARY.
(Erase heading not required.)

Army Form C. 2118.

Place	Date	Hour	Summary of Events and Information	Remarks and references to Appendices
In the Field	6/3/17		Section training continued throughout the Brigade – The G.O.C. inspected the Brigade horses accompanied by C.R.A. in afternoon.	
	7/3/17		Training continued in the morning – Football matches were played in the afternoon.	
	8/3/17		Section training continued, but was rather hampered by snow – bad weather.	
	9/3/17		Major General Franks, G.O.C. R.A. 2nd Army inspected the Batteries who continued with their Section training – Weather again very bad in the afternoon.	
	10/3/17		Inspections during the morning and football matches in the afternoon. 2nd Lieut Patterson joined 'B' Battery.	

March 1917

Page 3

112th Brigade RFA

WAR DIARY
or
INTELLIGENCE SUMMARY.

Army Form C. 2118.

Instructions regarding War Diaries and Intelligence Summaries are contained in F.S. Regs., Part II. and the Staff Manual respectively. Title pages will be prepared in manuscript.

Place	Date	Hour	Summary of Events and Information	Remarks and references to Appendices
In the field	1/3/17		Brigade Horse Show judged by the Brigade Major	
	2/3/17		Battery training, Harness & Signalling instruction carried out	
	3/3/17		Battery Training continued	
	4/3/17		Battery Training continued a football matches	
	5/3/17		Battery Training and Signalling instruction carried out	
	6/3/17		Battery Training and all day Signalling Scheme	
	7/3/17		Detailed Gas Officer for Gasdemonstration — Old Ranks being made to pass through gas cloud with small dose Respirators	
	8/3/17		Divisional Horse Show — 112 Bde took 3rd and numerous 2nd & 3rd	

March 1917 — Page 4
Army Form C. 2118.

112th Bde RFA

WAR DIARY
or
INTELLIGENCE SUMMARY.
(Erase heading not required.)

Place	Date	Hour	Summary of Events and Information	Remarks and references to Appendices
In The Field	19/3/17		Brigade Training Scheme at ETREHEM.	
	20/3/17		Preparation to moving from ESQUERDES.	
	21/3/17		Brigade marched at 11 am to billets 2 miles S.E. of BLARINGHEM.	
	22/3/17		Brigade continued march at 8.30 am to VIEUX BERQUIN.	
	23/3/17		Cleaning up billets etc.	
	24/3/17		Cleaning up and General fatigues.	
	25/3/17		Batteries moved to lines just EAST of Steenwerke — 46 L.D. & 2 changing round —	
	26/3/17		General fatigue — Column left at 9.15 am to reconnoitre position	

T2134. Wt. W708—776. 500000. 4/15. Sir J. C. & 8.

March 1917 page 5

112th Bde RFA

WAR DIARY
or
INTELLIGENCE SUMMARY.
(Erase heading not required.)

Army Form C. 2118.

Place	Date	Hour	Summary of Events and Information	Remarks and references to Appendices
In the field	27/3/17		Inspection of Brigade by II Army Commander on road South of Wagon Lines at 2 pm.	
"	28/3/17		Signalling instruction under Brigade Signal Officer carried out — General fatigues.	
	29/3/17		Signalling instruction continued and general fatigues	
	30/3/17		Signalling instruction carried out —	
	31/3/17		Signalling in morning — football in afternoon	

M.J.Moor Lieut Col.
Commanding 112th Bde RFA.

Army Form C. 2118

112TH BRIGADE R.F.A.

April 1917.

Vol / 8 Page 1

WAR DIARY or INTELLIGENCE SUMMARY

(Erase heading not required.)

Place	Date	Hour	Summary of Events and Information	Remarks and references to Appendices
In The Field.	April 1st 1917.		General Duties and fatigues at Wagon Lines - One Officer and 20 men per battery still working at STEENWERCK.	
-do-	2nd.		General duties and fatigues at Wagon Lines - One Officer and 20 men per battery still working at STEENWERCK.	
	3rd.		Colonel and Battery Commanders went over to NEUVE EGLISE to arrange details of relief of 1st N.Z.F.A. Bde.	
	4th.		Adjutant and Signals Officers proceeded to H.Q. 1st N.Z.F.A. Bde. One section of each Battery relieved one section of each Battery of the 1st N.Z.F.A. Bde. All exchanged guns except B/112 who had to bring in one section.	
	5th.		Remaining sections completed relief - All guns being exchanged. - Command passed to Colonel Ferman at 10.p.m. - At 12 midnight A/112 came tactically under the command of O.C. 3rd N.Z.F.A. Bde., and we covered 1 Battalion front (From U.15.a.1.2. to W-W Road with B, C, and D Batteries.)	
	6th.		Enemy shelled T.15.d. with about 250 - 4.2" and 5.9" between 8.a.m. and 9.30.a.m.	
	7th.		About 7.p.m. airfight between 8 of our machines and about 10 German scouts. One of our machines landed in our lines with observer killed and pilot wounded, another crashed in flames in our lines.	
	8th		Work still continuing on gun positions - About 200 rounds 5.9" (a few being gas) fired into N.32, 33, and T.2.	
	9th		Great VIMY offensive starts.	
	10th		2nd Lieut. BRUNNER J.M. joined the Brigade and was posted to "A" Battery - Weather very bad and snowy.	

Army Form C. 2118

April 1917
Page 2

112TH BRIGADE R.F.A.

WAR DIARY
or
INTELLIGENCE SUMMARY
(Erase heading not required.)

Place	Date	Hour	Summary of Events and Information	Remarks and references to Appendices
In The Field.	April 11th 1917.		Quiet day on this front - Snowed heavily all the afternoon - A little movement observed by HELL FARM.	
	12th.		Enemy Artillery exceptionally quiet - Our Artillery fired a little in registration and at noon "B" Battery shelled what seemed a camouflage trench from 0.25.a.9.0. to b.0.1. with 34 rounds.	
	13th.		"B" Battery fired about 100 rounds during the day - In the afternoon a balloon sheet on LUNN FARM was tried, but it was too windy. - "D" Battery calibrated their Hows: on HELL FARM - Enemy shelled T.3.a. and T.2.d. with 450 rds 4.2" and 100 rounds 5.9" during the morning.	
	14th.		Several German parties observed and fired on by our 18 pdrs - Enemy fire negligable.	
	15th.		Between 12 and 1. about 10 flashes were observed behind the crest at 0.26.d.0.1. - The ground behind this crest was searched by "B" Battery.	
	16th.		"D" Battery fired 107 rounds on hedge 0.31.b.6.8. to 7.6. to test effect by orders of C.R.A. Damage appeared slight. - Enemy Artillery quiet on our front. - Nothing of interest reported.	
	17th.		Bad visibility and much rain and snow - Nothing of interest reported.	
	18th.		Very bad visibility and everything very quiet.	
	19th.		Poor visibility - Wet day - Nothing to report - Quiet night and day.	
	20th.		Hostile Artillery fairly active about La PETITE MUNQUE Fm and C/112 in the evening - 110th Came in on our right, relieving 3rd Bde. N.Z.F.A. - About 9 pm.m. Gas Shells (LACHREMATORY) were fired on read behind C/112 - There was heavy firing from 7.30.p.m. to about 9.30.p.m. to our North near WYTSHAETE - Fine day - Hostile A.A. very active in the afternoon.	

Army Form C. 2118.

April 1917
Page 3

WAR DIARY
or
INTELLIGENCE SUMMARY.
(Erase heading not required.)

Instructions regarding War Diaries and Intelligence Summaries are contained in F.S. Regs., Part II. and the Staff Manual respectively. Title pages will be prepared in manuscript.

Place	Date	Hour	Summary of Events and Information	Remarks and references to Appendices
In the Field.	April 21st 1917.		Three Hostile observation balloon up S.E. of MESSINES. - D/112 report having seen 5.9" Battery firing behing ZAREEBA HEDGE at O.35.a.35.34. - Camouflage visible behind hedge - Battery engaged by D/112 - 3 Guns reported at U.3.b.3.4. muzzles seen under camouflage - Fine day - One of our huts and wireless knocked down by a shell 7.7.mm.	
	22nd.		An active day owing to the exceptionally good visibility - "C" Battery carried out a shoot with Balloon observation, HELL FARM, SWAYNES FARM, and 4 HUNS FARM being registered in this way. - "C" Battery also carried out an Aeroplane shoot - Batteries also shot on T.Ms, M.G. emplacements and suspected O.Ps - Altogther about 300 rounds 18 pdr and 74 rounds 4.5" were fired.	
	23rd.		Fine and bright - "B" Battery heavily shelled by 4.2. and 5.9. from 7.30.a.m. to about 8.45.a.m. Four gun pits knocked in, guns buried, no guns damaged. - Enemy planes very active from 6 to 9.a.m.	
	24th.		Fine and bright - Hostile Artillery quiet - T.Ms active on our trenches at 4.p.m. about N.36.c.c.9. cutting our wire. - Enemy reported massing opposite our left front N.36.central. at 7.p.m. - "B" and "C" Batteries fired some rounds on to this area. - All 3 Battery wires cut about 9.45.p.m. by some 6" Hows: thatv were moving out r running over our wires - Mended within 20 minutes - Enemy planes active from 6 to 9.a.m. 1 man killed and 2 wounded by "B" or "C" shots.	
	25th.		Low visibilty - "B" "C" and "D" Batteries wire cutting shoot at 4. to 4.35.p.m. N.35.central - two gaps cut. - Quiet night.	
	26th		A wire cutting and destructive shoot was carried out this afternoon between 4.55p.m. and 5.30.p.m. from N.36.d.23.73. to N.36.d.17.88. - 6.2" T.Ms and "C" Battery did the wire cutting with marked success. 180 Bombs were fired and 150 rounds A. ✱ At the same time D Battery with 6 How; fired 200 rounds on to the Support Trench.	
	27th		Nothing of interest happened - Enemy fairly quiet, but T.Ms fired a little in the Northern position of Sector. - Batteries fired in retalistion at request of Infantry.	
	28th.		Very successful wire cutting and destructive shoot carried out between 5.10 and 5.45.p.m. - on N.36.d.55.60. to N.36.d.75.00. - Wire and trenches badly blown about - 270 Bombs and 150 rounds 18 pdr were expended on the wire - 150 rounds 4.5" and 200 round 6" were also expended on trenches in rear.	

Army Form C. 2118.

WAR DIARY

~~INTELLIGENCE~~ SUMMARY

112TH BRIGADE R.F.A.

April 1917

Paget

(Erase heading not required.)

Instructions regarding War Diaries and Intelligence Summaries are contained in F. S. Regs., Part II. and the Staff Manual respectively. Title pages will be prepared in manuscript.

Place	Date	Hour	Summary of Events and Information	Remarks and references to Appendices
In the Field.	April 29th 1917.		At 3.15.a.m. all Batteries fired 2 rounds per gun per minute on front line which was reported full of Infantry - Received orders for relief at 1.p.m. - One section of each Battery Relieved by corrwsponding Batteries 175 Bde R.F.A. after dark.	
	30th.		A very heavy Bombardment on the Right commencing at 4.10.a.m. and lasting until 5.15.a.m. - Apparently raid at ST YVES - Though the bombardment extended further North - Support was given by this Brigade to the Group on the Right - Relief of the Brigade by the 175th Brigade R.F.A. completed - Fine day.	

Lieut. Col. R.F.A.
Commanding 112th Brigade R.F.A.

May 1917
Page 1

Army Form C. 2118.

WAR DIARY
or
INTELLIGENCE SUMMARY
(Erase heading not required.)

112th Brigade R.F.A.

Vol 19

Place	Date	Hour	Summary of Events and Information	Remarks and references to Appendices
In the Field.	May 1st 1917.		Brigade Headquarters marched to its old billets between NEUF BERQUIN and VIEUX BERQUIN, Batteries remained at there same wagon lines just South of STEENWERCK.	
	2nd.		Batteries started training at their wagon lines, Standing Gun Drill, Signalling, and Marching Drill forming part of the programme.	
	3rd.		Training as above continued, and drivers took horses out grazing. D/112 went for an all night scheme in FORET DE NIEPPE.	
	4th.		Training and Horse grazing continued.	
	5th.		Usual training - D.D.V.S. inspected Battery horses accompanied by G.O.C., R.A. at 2.30.p.m.	
	6th.		Training continued.	
	7th.		Training continued.	
	8th.		One Section per Battery relieved 175 Brigade in the WULVERGHEM Sector at 9.30.p.m.	
	9th.		Remaing sections of Batteries and B.H.Q. relieved 175 Brigade and Command passed at 11.p.m.	
	10th.		"B" Battery were shelled with 4.2"s from E. of MESSINES between 7.30. and 8.30.a.m. About 300 shells in all were fired but no damage done to guns or pits. One gunner wounded. Batteries re-registered and a certain amount of Hostile T.M. Fire was dealt with by HOWS;	
	~~11th.~~ 11th.		Lieut KNIGHT W. C/112 and Lieut HORNE D/112 recommenced work on positions for MAGNUM OPUS with 10 men per Battery.	
	12th.		A little hostile T.M. Activity on Battalion Front, our Batteries retaliated in every case and also fired on movement observed - Night firing on Paths and Tracks between 10.p.m. and 4.a.m.	

May 1917 Page 2

Army Form C. 2118.

WAR DIARY
or
INTELLIGENCE SUMMARY.

(Erase heading not required.)

112th Brigade R.F.A.

Instructions regarding War Diaries and Intelligence Summaries are contained in F. S. Regs., Part II. and the Staff Manual respectively. Title pages will be prepared in manuscript.

Place	Date	Hour	Summary of Events and Information	Remarks and references to Appendices
In the Field.	May 13th 1917.		From 5.p.m. to 5.45.p.m. a wire cutting shoot was carried out from U.1.a.0.8. to N.36.d.65.15 2" T.Ms fired 200 rounds on Front Line wire, 18 pdrs fired 600 rounds on wire in front of Support and the 4.5" Hows: fired 200 rounds on supports. A great deal of damage was done to the trenches and the wire was well cut. 300 rounds were fired by 18 pdrs on Paths and Tracks.	
	14th		A small wire cutting shoot carried out by C/112 in front of Southern portion of NUTMEG RESERVE with 600 rounds. The Hows fired 400 rounds on same trench with good effect. The shoot was done deliberately from 1.p.m. onwards. Night firing as on previous evening.	
	15th		Wire cutting carried out just N. of that done on the 13th by T.Ms, 18 pdrs, and 4.5"s with approximately same amount of ammunition. The wire again reported to have been well cleared and trenches very badly damaged. Night firing 300 rounds on Tracks etc by "C" Battery.	
	16th.		A raid was carried out by 13th Cheshires at MORTAR FARM covered by 112th Brigade, 175rd Bde, and 1st N.Z.F.A. Bde at 11.35.p.m. - 12 6" Hows and 8 2" T.Ms took part. At zero plus 2 a 'BOX' was formed and kept up till zero plus 20 afterc which the barrage expanded N.S.&E. and stopped at zero 25. No identifications were obtained but the German wire and trenches were found badly damaged.	
	17th.		Quiet during most of the day. - At 10.p.m. the R.I.R. attepmted a small raid on MORTAR FARM and a short Artillery programme was carried out consisting of a salvo at zero, 2 more at zero plus 3 and from zero plus 7 to zero plus 15 a small 'BOX' was formed. - No identifications were secured but the front line was found unoccupied.	
	18th.		"C" Battery cut wire in front of NUTMEG RESERVE with 400 rounds of "A" and "D" Battery bombarded UGLEY SUPPORT with 400 rounds with very good effect. In the evening a patrol of 2nd R.I.R. raided enemy and was helped to withdraw by Batteries forming a box round point of entry.	
	19th.		Very quiet day.	
	20th		At 1.a.m. an S.O.S. was reported opposite Right Battalion and our Batteries opened fire, it proved to be a false alarm. - AT 12 noon B.H.Q. moved to new Hqrs on WEST side of LINDENHOEK-NEUVE EGLISE ROAD - about half way between the two.	

May 1917
Page 25

Army Form C. 2118.

WAR DIARY
or
INTELLIGENCE SUMMARY.

(Erase heading not required.)

112TH BRIGADE R.F.A.

Instructions regarding War Diaries and Intelligence Summaries are contained in F. S. Regs., Part II. and the Staff Manual respectively. Title pages will be prepared in manuscript.

Place	Date	Hour	Summary of Events and Information	Remarks and references to Appendices
In the Field.	May 21st. 1917.		At 1.45. a call for help from xxx Group on our Left was received. "C" Battery switched on to their front and fired a few rounds, when to order to stop was received. A wire cutting and bombardment shoot on front line from N.36.a.60.20. to N.36.b.10.00. and support immediately in rear. 18 pdrs fired 600 rounds, 4.5' Hows: fired 200 rounds and 2" T.Ms 300. Great damage caused. The R.I.R. had a small raid and our guns were laid on a small box to extricate patrol., but this was not used as front trench and support was found to be unoccupied.	
	22nd.		"C" Battery fired 300 rounds, at wire in front of NUTMEG RESERVE and "D" Battery bombarded with 300 rounds at some screens on MESSINES RIDGE breeching them in several places. 1 Section of "B" 300 rounds fired by "A" Battery during the night on back ares. 1 Section of "A" and "B" went into their MAGNUM OPUS positions.	
	23rd.		Another wire cutting shoot and bombardment carried out at 5.p.m. 300 rounds 18 pdr and 300 4.5" and 300 T.M. bombs being fired. Night firing 300 rounds fired by "C" Battery. "A" and "B" completed move to MAGNUM OPUS positions and "D" Battery moved complete to theirs. - 3 Batteries of 2nd N.Z.F.A. Bde, replaced these on Bde Front until our own Batteries are shot in.	
	24th.		Wire cutting in front of NUTMEG RESERVE carried out by the Brigade - Ammunition 600 rounds.	
	25th.		Night of 25/26th - 50th Battery 34th Army Bde and A/93 Army Bde joined the group ʲ D/112 was transferred to "D" GROUP for tactics. Wire cutting was carried out in front of NUTMEG RESERVE - Night Firing was carried out on Roads tracks etc.	
	26th.		Wire cutting in front of NUTMEG RESERVE still being carried out - Night firing between 9.30.p.m. and 4.a.m. carried out on roads tracks etc.	
	27th.		Wire cutting still being continued - The enemys Artillery was active during the night Some H.E. and Gas Shells being fired into and along WULVERGHEM VALLEY. - 1 man was killed at Headquarters by an H.E. - this man belonged to the 3rd Section D.A.C.	

May 1917
page 4

Army Form C. 2118.

WAR DIARY
or
INTELLIGENCE SUMMARY

(Erase heading not required.)

Place	Date	Hour	Summary of Events and Information	Remarks and references to Appendices
In the Field.	May 28th. 1917.		Wire cutting was still continued in front of NUTMEG RESERVE - The enemy again shelled WULVERGHEM VALLEY and long the line during the night with Gas shells. Night firing carried out on Roads, tracks &c.	
	29th.		Wire cutting in front of NUTMEG RESERVE continued with - an aeroplane with 2 lights was seen very low over de KENNEBEK about 12 midnight. Night firing continued.	
	30th.		The Brigade continued to cut the wire in front of NUTMEG RESERVE, there was also a combined Wire cutting shoot by 2 Batteries at 5.p.m. - The enemy shelled DAYLIGHT CORNER with H.E. at 7.a.m. also some H.E. in WULVERGHEM VALLEY during the night.	
	31st.		Wire in front of NUTMEG RESERVE cut. - A practice barrage was carried out by the Group at 4.30.p.m. - The Wagon Lines of the Brigade were at DRANOUTRE were shelled at 4.a.m. - Several horses being killed and one Driver od D/112 was killed. Wagon lines moved to S.11.c.9.9. (Sheet 28.)	

(signature) Lieut. Col. R.F.A.
Commanding 112th Brigade R.F.A.

Army Form C. 2118.

WAR DIARY
or
INTELLIGENCE SUMMARY.

112Th Brigade R.F.A. June 1917.

(Erase heading not required.)

Instructions regarding War Diaries and Intelligence Summaries are contained in F.S. Regs., Part II. and the Staff Manual respectively. Title pages will be prepared in manuscript.

Place	Date	Hour	Summary of Events and Information	Remarks and references to Appendices
In The Field.	June 1st 1917.		Wire Cutting Carried out by the Brigade. Practice Barrage also carried out.	
	2nd.		Wire Cutting also 2 practice barrages. Raid at 10.50.p.m. - 11 Prisoners taken, continued until 1.50.a.m. We had 3 men slightly wounded. Heavy bombardment of MESSINES.	
	3rd.		Wire cutting also 2 practice barrages carried out at 11.30.a.m. and 3.15.p.m. Very fine and hot. Concentrated bombardment of WYTSCHEATE by Heavies at 11.a.m. and 3.p.m. - All heavies fired on WARNETON. Raid by the 1st Wilts South of MORTAR FARM - failed -.	
	4th.		Practice Barrage at 11.a.m. by arrangement with O.C. 36th Division. Right Group. Corps Practice Barrage for 25 minutes commencing at 1.45.p.m. - Weather and visibility very good. Hostile Artillery more active especially on HILL 63.	
	5th.		Army Practice barrage carried out at 3.p.m. lasting until 3.15.p.m. Simultaneously a small raid was carried out by 7th Infantry Brigade. - German Trenches were entered but no identifications were obtained. Heavy bombardment by Heavy Artillery.	
	6th		Few rounds fired on wire in front of NUTMEG and NATHAN RESERVE to prevent repair during the day. Headquarters Signaller wounded.	
	7th		Attack on MESSINE - New Zealand and MESSINES RIDGE - 25th Division. WYTSCHEATE - 36th Div. commenced at 3.10.a.m. and was entirely successful. All objectives were gained. - 25th head up for a short time at 4 HUNS FARM by Machine Guns - A good number of prisoners taken - Our Casualties believed to be comparatively slight. Green Line reached in the evening (OOSTRAVERNE LINE) 2 Counter attacks repulsed in the afternoon about 2.p.m. and 7.15.p.m. 25th Divl. Arty moved from de KENNEBAK position to our old support line in front of FORT PINKIE getting into action again about 12.30.p.m. and were able to assist in both counter attacks. German Artillery active all day shelling MESSINES and SLEPING ROOF FARM and all tracks leading up to them - 6 tanks seen in the afternoon near MESSINES. Major D.D.H. CAMPBELL, M.C. A/112 Killed with Corpl. J. HAYES Signaller between MESSINES and SWAYNES FARM. 2nd Lt. W.L. WILSON C/112 Gassed. A/112 had a Signaller wounded.	

Army Form C. 2118.

WAR DIARY
or
INTELLIGENCE SUMMARY
(Erase heading not required.)

112th Brigade R.F.A.

Place	Date	Hour	Summary of Events and Information	Remarks and references to Appendices
In the Field.	June 8th 1917		Desultory shelling of MESSINES and SWAYNES FARM - Extended our O.P. line to ridge beyond 4 HUNS FARM to a shell hole. - C/112 moved forward to position at about 400 yards West of 4 HUNS FARM at 6.30.p.m. - C/112 had 4 men slightly wounded by premature in rear.	
	9th.		D/112 moved up behind C/112 at 6.p.m. - C/112 had 1 man killed at Battery position by shell splinter.	
	10th.		2nd Lieut. G.M. FRASER wounded by sniper in back about 8.a.m. at O.P. - Enemy shelled chiefly round DESPAGNE FARM AND MESSINES.	
	11th.		"A" and "B" Batteries moved up into positions near "C" Battery during the evening. Three Hun planes flying very low over our trenches between DESPAGNE FARM and MESSINES. These were shot at by our Infantry, but were up from 5.p.m. to after 7.p.m. None of our planes took any notice of them although this was reported 3 or 4 times.	
	12th.		Headquarters moved up to South side of L'ENFER WOOD. One of our R.E.8. Planes shot down by Bosche plane about 8.40.a.m. - Plane fell in flames over MESSINES RIDGE apparently in our lines - At 12 noon we came under 4th Australian Division.	
	13th.		Patrols reported to be in GAPAARD - 2 7.7.c.m. Guns removed by B/112 (2nd. Lt. B. BEBBINGTON) to wagon lines from DESPAGNE FARM via WYTSCHAETE. Hostile Artillery fairly quiet, except for some heavy shells on MESSINES during the afternoon. STEIGNAST FARM shelled by D/112 from 7 to 7.30.p.m. with 100 rounds.	
	14th.		2nd. Lt. B. BEBBINGTON attempted to get remaining 2 7.7.c.m. guns away from DESPAGNE FARM at 3.a.m. but teams could not get through WYTSCHAETE owing to heavy shelling. 75th Inf. Bde - 25th Division attacked at 7.30.p.m. and gained all objectives just EAST of GAPAARD - All fire ceased at 9.30.p.m. - 7 Hostile planes flew very low over our lines at 8.p.m. firing at our Infantry, recrossing line several times	
	15th		2nd. Lt. B. BEBBINGTON got the remaining 2 7.7.c.m. guns out at 4.a.m. - Heavy firing just South of WARNETON from 8.p.m. to 9.30.p.m. - 1 man killed by shell splinter in D/112.	

Army Form C. 2118.

WAR DIARY
or
~~INTELLIGENCE~~ SUMMARY.

(Erase heading not required.)

112th Brigade R.F.A.

Page 3

Instructions regarding War Diaries and Intelligence Summaries are contained in F.S. Regs., Part II. and the Staff Manual respectively. Title pages will be prepared in manuscript.

June 1917

Place	Date	Hour	Summary of Events and Information	Remarks and references to Appendices
In the Field.	June 16th 1917.		NORMAL. - Hostile planes red fusilages flew as usual very low over our trenches about 7.30.p.m.	
	17th.		Brigade Front moved further South - Large fires seen about QUESNOY and WERVICQ. 7 Hostile planes (red fusilages-) were over again in the evening about 7.p.m. They brought down one of our planes F.E. in flames, but machine appeared to be under control disappearing beyond WYTSCHAETE. Enemy planes appear to be far superior to ours in speed and climbing powers. The Brigade had 9 Casualties - "A" Battery 5. "B" Battery 2. and "D" Battery 1 and 2nd Lieut J.V.D. Radford was wounded (8 Wounded and 1 Killed). At 11.p.m. bursts of shrapnel were fired over Batteries just West of L'ENFER WOOD and on L'ENFER WOOD.	
	18th		12.30.p.m. bursts of shrapnel over Batteries West side of L'ENFER WOOD and Brigade Headquarters and again at 3.p.m. also some 4.2"s - Rain and thunder about 3.30.p.m. - One of our planes a Nieupert was attacked by two enemy planes simultaneously. Eventually it escaped some F.Es coming to its rescue.	
	19th		1.a.m. - 3.30.a.m. very heavy shrapnel and H.E. fire on L'ENFER WOOD and South edge about 700 rounds fired. About 10.a.m. they put about 20 rounds of 5.9" in the wood one fell in "B" Btty's Coolhouse and killed 1 and wounded 2 others. The Brigade had 7 Casualties. A 14.c.m. H.V. Gun fires from about P.28.c. - All the guns with the exception of a 4.2" Btty which fires from HOUTHEM fire from direction of MESSINES. Brigade Headquarters moved out of the wood to N.36.c.75.75. - "A" Battery moved 1 section to new position about 400ˣ South. "B" Battery making new positions, about 500ˣ further South. - 2 Balloons brought down by BOSCHE planes.	
	20th.		Barrages enemy's front defences at 3.a.m. - A gged many were hit running from shell hole to shell hole. - Hostile Artillery active during the day firing on his old front line in front of FORT PINKIE.	
	21st.		"D" Battery had 2 men killed and 6 wounded and 3 horses killed and several wounded by 1 shell between 10.p.m. and 11.p.m. - "A" Battery moved to new position.	

2353 Wt. W2544/1454 700,000 5/15 D. D. & L. A.D.S.S./Forms/C. 2118.

Army Form C. 2118.

WAR DIARY
or
INTELLIGENCE-SUMMARY.
(Erase heading not required.)

June 1917 112 Brigade. Page 4

Place	Date	Hour	Summary of Events and Information	Remarks and references to Appendices
In The Field.	June 22nd. 1917.		Enemy Planes very active especially in the evening - They were not interfered with by any of our planes.	
	23rd.		Enemy planes active as usual in the afternoon and evening. None of our planes interfered with them.	
	24th.		3 of our observation balloons brought down in the morning and 2 in the afternoon by hostile planes.	
	25th.		Another balloon brought down by hostile planes - Enemy balloon was brought down in the morning. 2 of our planes brought down by hostile planes in the enemy's lines.	
	26th.		Quiet day for all Batteries. - Another of our planes brought down - 2 German planes attacked 11 of our planes in the afternoon.	
	27th.		At 3.p.m. one of our balloons was brought down in flames by enemy aircraft - Enemy aircraft was very active in evening. A triplane brought down a Red ALBATROSS in the enemy's lines at 8.30.a.m. - "B" Battery had 2 guns hit.	
	28th.		3.a.m. "B" Battery were shelled while getting a gun out - 1 Section moved to 18th Btty (6th Aus) position at 2.a.m. "C" Battery were shelled by 5.9" and the area around the Battery. Very Heavy thunderstorm at 9.p.m.	
	29th.		"B" Battery moved two guns to 18th Battery position (6th Aus) near GABIAN FARM, WULVERGHEM - MESSINES Road shelled intermittently all day. We got our anti aircraft gun in position and fired 6 rounds at enemy planes flying very low. At 8.30.p.m. enemy planes 8. Chased 4 of our Triplanes as far back as WULVERGHEM before they gave up the chase. Enemy planes over our lines most of the afternoon. at 11.p.m. havy firing about 2 or 3 miles to the North of our zone.	
	~~30th.~~ ~~30th.~~ 30th.		S.O.S. at 1.10.a.m. and 1.20.a.m. on our zone - There was no attack. - At 1.a.m. "B" Btty got into action near GABIAN FARM.	

Major R.F.A.
Commanding 112th Brigade R.F.A.

Army Form C. 2118.

WAR DIARY
or
INTELLIGENCE SUMMARY
(Erase heading not required.)

112th Brigade R.F.A.   Vol 22

Instructions regarding War Diaries and Intelligence Summaries are contained in F.S. Regs., Part II. and the Staff Manual respectively. Title pages will be prepared in manuscript.

Place	Date	Hour	Summary of Events and Information	Remarks and references to Appendices
In the Field.	1st Aug. 1917.		Normal day - B.H.Q. in the RAMPARTS YPRES, Batteries in action under O.C. C GROUP ARTILLERY.	
	2nd.		The Brigade had 40 Casualties - D/112 having 31 of these. Batteries still in action under the Group.	
	3rd.		Headquarters moved out of the ramparts to Forward W.Ls BELGIAN CHATEAU owing to 74th Inf Bde coming in. A draft of 16 received for the Brigade. Batteries still in action under the group.	
	4th.		The Brigade had 6 casualties. B.H.Q. at F.W.L. - Batteries still in action under Group.	
	5th.		2nd Lieut M.G. DURNFORD reported as missing with a Gunner Chipperfield. - BH.Q. at Forward W.L. Batteries still in action.	
	6th.		H.Q. and W.Ls less 60 horses moved back to rear W.Ls. "D" Battery had 4 wounded and 1 killed on arriving in rear Lines by an hostile shell.	
	7th.		Batteries in action under group. 3 Casualties reported. A draft of 61 received and posted to Batteries.	
	8th.		Batteries in action under Group - B.H.Q. at Rear Wagon Lines.	
	9th.		Batteries in action under Group - B.H.Q. at Rear Wagon Lines.	
	10th.		Batteries continue to be in action under "C" Group. - A draft of 5 N.C.Os received.	
	11th.		Batteries still in action under the group. - The Brigade was allotted 300 baths at HALIFAX CAMP.	
	12th.		B.H.Q. at Rear Wagon Lines - Batteries still in action.	
	13th.		Nothing to report - Batteries still in action, B.H.Q. at Rear Wagon Lines.	

Army Form C. 2118.

WAR DIARY
or
INTELLIGENCE SUMMARY. 112th Brigade R.F.A.

(Erase heading not required.)

Instructions regarding War Diaries and Intelligence Summaries are contained in F.S. Regs., Part II. and the Staff Manual respectively. Title pages will be prepared in manuscript.

Place	Date	Hour	Summary of Events and Information	Remarks and references to Appendices
In the Field.	14th.		On the Night 14th/15th Batteries came out of action to Rear W.L. Forward W.L.s moved back to Rear W.L.s - 2nd Lieut F.J.B. GARDNER awarded the MILITARY CROSS.	
	15th.		The Brigade moved at 2.p.m. to CANADA CORNER - CURRAGH CAMP. - 1 man of "A" Battery and 1 man of "C" Battery awarded the M.M. and D.C.M. respectively.	
	16th.		General cleaning up and fatigues at the New camp.	
	17th.		General duties and Gun Drill carried out.	
	18th		General duties and Gun Drill carried out.	
	19th		Brigade still at CURRAGH CAMP - Baths allotted at LA CLYTTE for 320 men.	
	20th		General duties and Gun Drill - Arrangements being made to hold Brigade Sports on the 21st.	
	21st.		Brigade moved at 8.a.m. to Rear W.L. at G.18.c. (Sheet 28) - Sports cancelled.	
	22nd.		General duties and fatigues carried out.	
	23rd.		Brigade moved at 9.a.m. to Wagon Lines at OUDERZEELE. - Sports again cancelled.	
	24th.		Brigade returned at 4.p.m. to Rear W.L.s in G.18.c. arriving there at 9.30.p.m.	
	25th.		General Duties and fatigues carried out.	
	26th		Church Parade at 9.30.a.m. - Received orders to prepare positions East of former positions.	
	27th		O.C. and B.Cs rode out at 5.a.m. to chose positions - Very heavy rain.	
	28th		1 Section per Battery went into action - D/112 only 2 guns.	
	29th		Remainder of Batteries went in - D/112 1 gun - Guns registered A/112 had one wounded.	

Army Form C. 2118.

WAR DIARY
or
~~INTELLIGENCE SUMMARY~~ 112th Brigade R.F.A.

(Erase heading not required.)

Instructions regarding War Diaries and Intelligence Summaries are contained in F.S. Regs., Part II. and the Staff Manual respectively. Title pages will be prepared in manuscript.

Place	Date	Hour	Summary of Events and Information	Remarks and references to Appendices
In the Field	Aug ~~29th~~ 30th 1917		Headquarters took over Headquarters LILLE GATE – A/112 had 1 wounded – C/112 had 1 killed and 4 wounded – Guns registered.	
	31st		Corps G.O.C., R.A. visited Headquarters – C/112 had 2 wounded and B/112 1 wounded. Col. E.V. SARSON took over "D" GROUP ARTILLERY at 12 noon. – "D" GROUP consisting of 112th Brigade R.F.A. and 38th A.F.A. Brigade½	

M.Sain Lieut. Col. R.F.A.

Commanding 112th Brigade R.F.A.

Army Form C. 2118.

WAR DIARY
or
INTELLIGENCE SUMMARY.   112th Brigade R.F.A.   Vol 23

(Erase heading not required.)

Instructions regarding War Diaries and Intelligence Summaries are contained in F. S. Regs., Part II. and the Staff Manual respectively. Title pages will be prepared in manuscript.

Place	Date	Hour	Summary of Events and Information	Remarks and references to Appendices
In the Field.	Sept 1st 1917.		Usual Harrassing fire carried out - Enemy planes very active. Battery positions intermittently shelled during morning in I.11.c. and I.17.b.	
	2nd.		Usual harassing fire carried out - Enemy planes very active.	
	3rd.		Usual harassing fire carried out - Enemy planes very active flying very low over Battery positions.	
	4th.		"D" Group became "C" Group - Enemy planes very active.	
	5th.		Usual harassing fire carried out - Enemy Planes very active flying very low early morning,	
	6th.		Batteries shelled intermittently all day in I.11.c. and I.17.b. - 2 Machine Guns posted near Battery positions to keep off low flying E.A. - Smoke barrage by "C" Group 7.15. - 8.55.a.m.	
	7th.		Quiet day - Usual harassing fire carried out.	
	8th.		Quiet day - A few gas shells during morning and afternoon in back areas MENIN ROAD and ZILLEBEKE LAKE - Usual harassing fire carried out.	
	9th.		About 4.a.m. Battery positions by BIRR CROSS ROADS were heavily shelled by Gas Shell. "D" Battery shelled with 8" during the evening - NO damage. 2 Guns damaged by stray shells -	
	10th.		Battery positions in I.11.c. very heavily shelled from 6.30.a.m. to 11.30.a.m. with 5.9" and 4.2" - There being as many as 40 rounds in the minute from the direction of BECELAERE. Batteries handed over 1 section to the 5th Australian F.A. Bde.	
	11th.		Relief of Batteries completed - Quiet day on the front.	
	12th		H.Q. handed over to H.Q. 8th Aus: F.A. Bde and proceeded to W.L. at 7.30.a.m. - Brigade marched to EECKE area leaving at 4.p.m. - All batteries in by 8.p.m. - Batteries handed over to I.O.M. all pieces and breech screws and retained carriages and stores only.	

Army Form C. 2118.

WAR DIARY
or
INTELLIGENCE SUMMARY.   112th Brigade R.F.A.

(Erase heading not required.)

Instructions regarding War Diaries and Intelligence Summaries are contained in F. S. Regs., Part II. and the Staff Manual respectively. Title pages will be prepared in manuscript.

Place	Date	Hour	Summary of Events and Information	Remarks and references to Appendices
In the Field.	Sept. 13th 1917		General fatigues – Cleaning up – Laying and fuze setting.	
	14th		General duties carried out in EECKE AREA. – Laying and fuze setting.	
	15th		General Fatigues and cleaning up – Laying and fuze setting.	
	16th		Brigade marched to WITTES arriving at 11.30.a.m.	
	17th		Brigade marched from WITTES to AMETTES arriving at 12 noon. Brigade Headquarters at AMES.	
	18th		General Fatigues – Preparations for sports.	
	19th		General fatigues – –do–	
	20th		General fatigues – –do–	
	21st		Preparations for sports – Brigade Pulled 110th Brigade – TUG OF WAR and lost.	
	22nd.		Preparations for sports – Shooting on range.	
	23rd½		Training on range – Shooting etc.	
	24th		Divisional Artillery Sports.	
	25th		Training and shooting on range.	
	26th		Divisional Fete at ALOUAGNE – 112th Brigade took 7 prizes. – Major W.G. MACKAY, M.C. took over command of the Brigade – Colonel SARSON, going on leave.	
	27th		General fatigues and cleaning up in the AMETTES AREA.	

Army Form C. 2118.

WAR DIARY
or
INTELLIGENCE SUMMARY.

112th Brigade R.F.A.

(Erase heading not required.)

Instructions regarding War Diaries and Intelligence Summaries are contained in F.S. Regs., Part II. and the Staff Manual respectively. Title pages will be prepared in manuscript.

Place	Date	Hour	Summary of Events and Information	Remarks and references to Appendices
In The Field	Sept 28th 1917		Advance parties of 1 Officer, 1 N.C.O., and 2 Signallers per Battery and B.H.Q. left for new positions by motor lorry.	
	29th		Advance billeting parties left for FOSSE 10 at 9.a.m.	
	30th		Brigade left AMETTES AREA and marched to FOSSE 10 arriving about 3.p.m.	

[signature] Major R.F.A.
Commanding 112th Brigade R.F.A.

Army Form C. 2118.

WAR DIARY
or
INTELLIGENCE SUMMARY.

112TH BRIGADE R.F.A.

(Erase heading not required.)

Instructions regarding War Diaries and Intelligence Summaries are contained in F.S. Regs., Part II. and the Staff Manual respectively. Title pages will be prepared in manuscript.

Place	Date	Hour	Summary of Events and Information	Remarks and references to Appendices
In The Field.	Oct 1st 1917		Relief of Brigade completed during night - H.Qrs taken over at 9.p.m. - Enemy T.Ms active during night.	
	2nd.		Quiet day. T.Ms active during night.	
	3rd.		Quiet day - A few shells put into LIEVIN during the morning - T.Ms active during the morning 9.2" engaged 2 T.M.s in the afternoon.	
	4th.		Heavy firing on the South of Lens. - Batteries fired at slow rate on S.O.S. lines between 7.p.m. and 9.45.p.m. when everything was reported quiet. Enemy T.ms quiet during day. "B" Battery had a direct hit on their ration wagon near H.qrs ; 1 man killed 1 missing, 2 horses killed and 1 wounded. "C" Battery - 2nd Lieut M.C. Kay wounded and 4 men badly burnt owing to ammunition in pit being set on fire by shell - 2nd Lieut M.C. Kay recommended for coolness in taking 3 men from burning ammunition and attempting to put out fire. "C" Battery had 1 gun put out of action by direct hit.	
	5th.		Cross roads by H.Qrs shelled by 4.2" and 7.7.m.m. during the morning. - LEIVIN was shelled intermittently during the day. 60th Battery C.F.A. in M.16.c. had about 50 4.2"s round about their position and some ammunition blown up. Gas was released by us at 3.30.a.m. into railway cutting just North of LENS.	
	6th.		1 Section relieved during night and returned to Wagon Lines.	
	7th.		Rest of Brigade (2 sections per Battery) relieved and returned to Wagon Lines.	
	8th.		General Fatigues and cleaning up - 1 Section per Battery relieve 1 section 41st Bde R.F.A. (Less "B" Battery) O.C. Brigade visited new positions. - H.Qrs Brigade moved to Billets in BETHUNE for night at Infantry Barracks. 2 sections per Battery relieved remaining 2 sections of 41st Bde in action.	

Army Form C. 2118.

WAR DIARY
or
INTELLIGENCE SUMMARY   112TH BRIGADE R.F.A.

(Erase heading not required.)

Instructions regarding War Diaries and Intelligence Summaries are contained in F.S. Regs., Part II. and the Staff Manual respectively. Title pages will be prepared in manuscript.

Place	Date	Hour	Summary of Events and Information	Remarks and references to Appendices
In the Field.	Oct 9th 1917		Headquarters moved up and took over new H.Qrs. - S.O.S. sent up by PORTUGUESE on Left - There was no attack.	
	10th		Registration carried out.	
	11th		Very Quiet - Nothing to report.	
	12th		Registration of Batteries carried out. - Batteries commence carting shale to W.Ls and improving standings etc.	
	13th		Very Quiet.	
	14th		Very quiet.	
	15th		Very quiet - Nothing to report.	
	16th		-do-	
	17th		General Fatigues in Wagon Lines - Carting shale and material for gun Positions.	
	18th		General Fatigues. Quiet Day.	
	19th		General Fatigues in Wagon Lines. - Carting Shale for Horse Standings and material for Gun positions. -do-	
	20th		General duties still being carried out.	
	21st		General Fatigues at the Wagon Lines - Quiet day.	
	22nd.		Adjutant and Signal Officer proceed on leave - General duties being carried out.	
	23rd.		"B" Battery Marching Order parade - General duties being carried out.	

Army Form C. 2118.

WAR DIARY
or
INTELLIGENCE-SUMMARY.
(Erase heading not required.)

112th Brigade R.F.A.

Instructions regarding War Diaries and Intelligence Summaries are contained in F. S. Regs., Part II. and the Staff Manual respectively. Title pages will be prepared in manuscript.

Place	Date	Hour	Summary of Events and Information	Remarks and references to Appendices
In the Field.	24th Oct 1917.		Rumours of intended raid from prisoner - "C" Battery marching order parade.	
	25th	4.45.a.m.	attempted raid by enemy opposite Right Sector.	
		11.5.a.m.	Wire cutting on 110th Brigade Zone.	
			"D" Battery marching order parade.	
		8.30.p.m.	T.Ms gassed AUCHY Area.	
	26th		General fatigues at W.Ls - Carting shale etc.	
	27th		General duties still being carried out.	
	28th		G.O.C. Division inspected W.Ls of the Brigade.	
	29th		Usual Wagon line fatigues - Carting shale etc.	
	30th		Rain. Usual W.L. fatigues. - Testing S.O.S. Rockets at 8.p.m.	
	31st.	10.40.a.m.	An ALBATROSS D.3. shot down one of our ARMSTRONG WHITWORTH in flames falling into the enemy lines.	
		3.20.p.m.	One of our balloons near LOCON shot down by E.A. - E.A. returned to its lines apparently untouched.	
		6.2.p.m.	CLOUD GAS reported G.1. and CANAL LEFT by Right Battalion. No enemy fire. Batteries stopped firing at 6.40.p.m.	

W Thom Lieut. Col. R.F.A.
Commanding 112th Brigade R.F.A.

Army Form C. 2118.

WAR DIARY
or
INTELLIGENCE SUMMARY

(Erase heading not required.)

112th Brigade R.F.A.

Place	Date	Hour	Summary of Events and Information	Remarks and references to Appendices
In the Field.	Nov 1st 1917		Batteries registered points on wire for following shoots on 2nd 3rd 4th insts	
	2nd.		Batteries wire cutting in A.3.d. Enemy retaliated with 5.9" 4.2" and 7.7mm. and T.M. in A.3.c. and GIVENCHY.	
	3rd.		Wire cutting 9.45.a.m. - Retaliation about 500 rounds 7.7.mm. in A.3.c and A.9.b.	
	4th		Wire cutting and bombardment of same points as above. Hostile retaliation was heavy on front line and support during hours of shoot.	
	5th		Batteries fired in retaliation to hostile trench mortars and shell fire at different times during day. Visibility was bad and no movement was observed.	
	6th		A quiet day. A little retaliation was carried out on enemy trenches at 10.15.p.m. gas was projected on the enemy by the Brigade on our right.	
	7th		A wire cutting shoot was carried out by T.Ms and the Brigade on our right in which we co-operated from 11.a.m. to 12.30.p.m. Our 18 pounders fired 900 rounds and our hows 4.5" In the afternoon a bombardment by heavies 4.5" H.T.Ms were carried out on hostile front line trench on either side of the canal to break up suspected gas cylinders there. Bombardment lasted from 3.30. to 4.30.p.m. 18 pounders barraged C.Ts during this shoot.	
	8th		Wire cutting on CANAL and CAMBRIN sectors continued assisted by us. Gaps were reported to have been cut and wire much damaged. A bombardment by heavies, Hows , H.T.Ms were carried out in the afternoon on german front line just astride the canal as gas was reported to be installed there. Trenches were much damaged. Night firing was carried out to keep wire open.	

Army Form C. 2118.

WAR DIARY
or
~~INTELLIGENCE SUMMARY~~

(Erase heading not required.)

112th Brigade R.F.A.

Instructions regarding War Diaries and Intelligence Summaries are contained in F. S. Regs., Part II. and the Staff Manual respectively. Title pages will be prepared in manuscript.

Place	Date	Hour	Summary of Events and Information	Remarks and references to Appendices
In the Field.	Nov. 9th 1917.		Uneventful day and very bad weather. Night firing was carried out to keep open the wire that had been cut during previous few days shoots.	
	10th		"B" Battery personnel took over guns and positions from "A" Battery who withdrew to wagon lines Quiet day and heavy rain during afternoon. 75th Infantry Brigade on CANAL Sector made a raid without result. We fired a few rounds in support.	
	11th		"B" and "C" Batteries fired 50 and 100 rounds respectively to destroy further the damaged wire in front of Right Battalion. Night firing was carried out - 50 rounds each by "B" and "C" on wire and communications. Silent raid carried out by 10th Cheshires failed to get identifications and had no casualties.	
	12th		"D" Battery fired 200 rounds EX and 2" T.Ms 62 rounds and 6" Newtons 34 rounds on new hostile work behind E SAP. Numerous direct hits obtained. Enemy reported to have registered with "MINNIES" and 4.2"s on extreme N of our sector. Raid was thought possible.	
	13th		Quiet day. Visibility bad "D" Battery fired on a T.M. opposite Left Battalion with good results Major W.G. McKAY also engaged a T.M. with 6" hows.	
	14th		Quiet day. - During night the PORTUGUESE were to have carried out a raid assisted by s ome guns of this Group, but this was cancelled just before zero hour.	
	15th		Nothing to report - 18 pounders were inactive. - Hows fired 20 rounds on a hostile Battery, 20 more on T.M. and 15 on working party - Usual night firing carried out.	
	16th		Very misty day and visibility very bad - Hostile artillery inactive and so was ours.	
	17th		"B" and "C" Batteries carried out minor shoot on wire between SUNKEN ROAD and A.3.b.4.8. to further damage it. 50 rounds per Battery being fired - Usual night firing programme being carried out.	

Army Form C. 2118.

WAR DIARY
or
INTELLIGENCE SUMMARY. 112th Brigade R.F.A.

(Erase heading not required.)

Instructions regarding War Diaries and Intelligence Summaries are contained in F. S. Regs., Part II. and the Staff Manual respectively. Title pages will be prepared in manuscript.

Place	Date	Hour	Summary of Events and Information	Remarks and references to Appendices
In the Field.	18th Nov. 1917.		Left Battalion were rather troubled with T.Ms on extreme N of our sector. Retaliation was brought to bear with 18 pounders and 4.5"s and 6" and a definite shoot was arranged for the next morning. Night firing targets were changed to different communication trenches.	
	19th		6" hows fired 100 rounds on front line opposite extreme N of our sector assisted by H.T.Ms "B" and "C" each fired 100 rounds on the wire and "D" and "C" took on trench mortars with good effect causing 2 explosions. Night firing was carried out as above.	
	20th		A good deal of movement was observed in A.11.a. on light railway and fired on with good result From 3 to 3.45.pm. a shoot by heavies T.Ms abd 4.5"s combined with 18 pounders was carried out Hostile retaliation was very heavy for 15 minutes just after finish of shoot.	
	21st		Quiet day with drizzle and poor visibility, However some movement was observed about A.5.a.50.75. and fired on.	
	22nd.		Quiet day - Batteries fired on movement and did usual night firing but no organised shoot took place.	
	23rd.		General KIRWAN G.O.C. R.A. X1 Corps inspected Batteries, Quiet day and batteries sniped usual movement	
	24th	Owing	A combined shoot took place between 2 and 2.45.p.m. with T.Ms and heavies on T.Ms in front of CANADIAN ORCHARD and on mine shaft opposite E. SAP - Hostile retaliation slight at night. owing to a suspected Hostile raid all guns were laid on the left of our sector.	
	25th		Quiet day Usual sniping of movement and night firing carried out.	
	26th		During the afternoon "C" Battery sniping gun had 500 5.9"s and 4.2"s at them without damage being done to equipment and personnel.	

Army Form C. 2118.

WAR DIARY
or
INTELLIGENCE SUMMARY. 112th Brigade R.F.A.
(Erase heading not required.)

Instructions regarding War Diaries and Intelligence Summaries are contained in F. S. Regs., Part II. and the Staff Manual respectively. Title pages will be prepared in manuscript.

Place	Date	Hour	Summary of Events and Information	Remarks and references to Appendices
In the Field	27th Nov. 1917.		"C" Battery moved their sniping gun to a position in the same neighbourhood and registered it. Usual night firing – 7th I.B. were relieved by 127th L.B.	
	28th		Very quiet day – Little hostile shelling reported on this front. No night firing was carried out tonight.	
	29th		Advanced parties from 211th Bde R.F.A. 42nd Div came over to start taking over positions. Good visibility and hostile aircraft were active flying at great heights. BETHUNE was shelled at intervals during the day.	
	30th.		Hostile aircraft active - Heavy shelling S. of our front during afternoon and night Relieve of 42nd Div commenced 24 hours earlier than originally ordered.	

Lieut. Col. R.F.A.
Commanding 112th Brigade R.F.A.

Army Form C. 2118.

WAR DIARY
or
INTELLIGENCE-SUMMARY.
(Erase heading not required.)

Instructions regarding War Diaries and Intelligence Summaries are contained in F.S. Regs., Part II. and the Staff Manual respectively. Title pages will be prepared in manuscript.

Place	Date	Hour	Summary of Events and Information	Remarks and references to Appendices
In the Field.	Dec 1st 1917		Relief by 211th Bde 42nd D.A. completed, B.H.Q. and "C" and "D" Batteries moved to VENDIN, "A" and "B" Batteries to ANNEZIN.	
	2nd.		Cleaning up and awaiting orders to move. Very cold weather.	
	3rd.		Orders received for entraining for 3rd Army Area. Batteries got ready to move.	
	4th		B.H.Q. entrained at BETHUNE and Batteries followed at 3 hours interval.	
	5th		B.H.Q. detrained at BOISLEUX AU MONT by 2.a.m. and marched to tents at COURCELLES arriving at 5.a.m. Batteries reached camp at 3 hours intervals afterwards. Very hard cold weather. Colonel and B.Cs proceeded to reconnoitre in the VI Corps MORCHIES AREA, 1 section of each Battery relieved 1 section of 281 Bde under 3rd D.A. during the night.	
	6th.		Remaining sections relieved the 281 Bde and B.H.Q. took over Group comprising 112th and 110th Brigades.	
	7th.		Batteries registered and got to know the country. 25th Division Infantry took over part of front.	
	8th.		Quiet day with bad weather and visibility.	
	9th.		110th Bde R.F.A. formed Right Group of 25th Div Front from 6.p.m. 112th new cover 74th Inf Bde 110th new cover 7th Inf Bde. B.H.Q. had one man wounded.	
	10th		25th Division and 25th D.A. took over command of portion of the line held by 25th Divn. Very clear visibility. A/293 and D/293 started reconnoitering positions to come in to 112th Brigade Group. Great aeroplane activity on both sides.	
	11th.		Night firing carried out as usual - Nothing to report of interest.	
	12th.		Bombardment of NO MANS LAND at 6.15.a.m. and 7.a.m. by Batteries in hopes of catahing enemy assembled for anticipated attack. Very great hostile aircraft activity. Enemy attacked and captured front line in the neighbourhood of BULLECOURT on short front.	

Army Form C. 2118.

WAR DIARY
or
INTELLIGENCE-SUMMARY.

112th Brigade R.F.A.

(Erase heading not required.)

Place	Date	Hour	Summary of Events and Information	Remarks and references to Appendices
In the Field.	Dec 13th 1917		Bombardment of NO MANS LAND and Front line trenches carried out again at 6.30.a.m. and 7.15.a.m. Very bad visibility. Night firing on approaches to QUEANT and PRONVILLE.	
	14th		Quiet day. Usual day and night harrassing fire carried out.	
	15th.		Very good visibility all day and much aircraft activity on both sides. Nothing eventful happened except Brigade covered by us extended its front slightly to the left.	
	16th.		Very cold day with snow showers and bad visibility. Usual day and night harrassing fire.	
	17th.		18 pounders fired 120 rounds by day and 240 rounds by night in occupied areas and traffic routes Hostile artillery and aircraft were very active.	
	18th.		18 pounder fired 84x rounds by day and 304 rounds by night and Hows 35 rounds by day and 135 rounds by night on usual tender spots. Slight hostile artillery activity. Hostile aircraft active in the forenoon.	
	19th.		A quiet day usual day and night firing, but nothing of interest to report.	
	20th.		18 pounders fired 350 rounds and hows 120 rounds during the 24 hours on likely targets and occupied areas. Visibility was very bad abad aircraft inactive.	
	21st.		Nothing to report except usual day and night shoots.	
	22nd.		Observation was good and a great deal of registration was carried out. 18 pounders fired 500 rounds during 24 hours and hows over 100. Hostile artillery also appeared to be doing some registration. Hostile aircraft and balloons were active.	
	23rd.		18 pounders fired 250 rounds in registration and hows 45 rounds. Usual day and night firing was carried out. Hostile Artillery was very quiet.	

Army Form C. 2118.

WAR DIARY
or
INTELLIGENCE-SUMMARY.

112th Brigade R.F.A.

(Erase heading not required.)

Place	Date	Hour	Summary of Events and Information	Remarks and references to Appendices
In the Field	Dec 24th 1917		During the past week the weather had been exceptionally severe, but a slight thaw set in to-day which only lasted till the next morning early. Ours did ordinary day and night tasks. Hostile Artillery again unusually quiet.	
	25th		Day and night firing was carried out as usual. Hostile Artillery also did a certain amount of day firing on LAGNICOURT and vicinity. Heavy snow during the night.	
	26th		Severe weather continued. A little hostile movement was observed and fired on. Visibility was good and aircraft active during the afternoon.	
	27th		No day or night firing tasks were allotted for to-day owing to the snow. Visibility was bad. One E.A. flew over our trenches for one hours in the morning and again in the afternoon.	
	28th		No day firing but 144 rounds 18 pounder were fired in harassing fire under orders from D.A. A german aeroplane was brought down near BEUGNY.	
	29th		Quiet day - Nothing to report. Slight thaw set in with heavy mist and bad visibility.	
	30th		Nothing to report - very bad visibility.	
	31st		Bad visibility again. Nothing to report - Frosty weather returns.	

Lieut. Col. R.F.A.
Commanding 112th Brigade R.F.A.

Army Form C. 2118.

WAR DIARY
or
INTELLIGENCE SUMMARY

112th Brigade R.F.A.

(Erase heading not required.)

Instructions regarding War Diaries and Intelligence Summaries are contained in F.S. Regs., Part II. and the Staff Manual respectively. Title pages will be prepared in manuscript.

Place	Date	Hour	Summary of Events and Information	Remarks and references to Appendices
In the Field.	Jan 1st 1918.		Observation poor - Enemy registered his own trenches with 4.2" in the BIRDCAGE. Aircraft inactive.	
	2nd.		Observation very fair - Considerable movement seen in PRONVILLE. 18 pounders fired on Corps concentration Cross Roads N.E. of PRONVILLE. Hostile guns quiet - Enemy aircraft fairly active over our lines.	
	3rd.		Observation fair - "B" and "C" Batteries on night firing - Some movement seen near SHRINE S of PRONVILLE. - Enemy guns quiet. 1 of our planes flew at low altitude between QUEANT and BULLECOURT for 2 hows - E.A. inactive.	
	4th.		Observation fair - "D" Battery registered by aeroplane, shoot unsuccessful. "A" and "C" Batteries shot on Corps concentration D.12.s.2.1. at 6.10.p.m. Enemy guns quiet. - A 5.9" fired on PRONVILLE. - "A" Battery fired on trenches opposite the NEST and BIRDCAGE during movement in PRONVILLE. Aircraft fairly active on both sides.	
	5th.		Observation poor - 18 pounders carried out night harassing fire - "A" Battery fired on trenches opposite the NEST and BIRDCAGE during the day. Aircraft inactive.	
	6th.		Observation poor - "D" Battery tried to register by aeroplane, nearly all rounds unobserved. 18 pounders carried out night harassing fire. - aircraft inactive.	
	7th.		Observation bad - 18 pdrs carried out night firing - Enemy guns quiet on Div Front - Heavy firing hea rd to the North near BULLECOURT at 4.45.p.m. - 1 E.A. flew very low over trenches N.E. of LAGNICOURT at 2.p.m., engaged without success by M.G's.	
	8th.		Observation bad,(snow) Hostile fire below normal - Our guns carried out night harassing fire.	
	9th.		Observation good up to 2.p.m. then snow - Our guns carried out night harassing fire. Hostile fire slightly above normal - Working parties fired on near PRONVILLE.	
	10th.		Observation good - Working parties near PRONVILLE - Hostile fire above normal - about 150 5.9" and 4.2" - aircraft fairly active on both sides.	

Army Form C. 2118.

WAR DIARY
or
INTELLIGENCE SUMMARY.   112th Brigade R.F.A.
(Erase heading not required.)

Instructions regarding War Diaries and Intelligence Summaries are contained in F.S. Regs., Part II. and the Staff Manual respectively. Title pages will be prepared in manuscript.

Place	Date	Hour	Summary of Events and Information	Remarks and references to Appendices
In the Field.	11th Jan 1918.		Observation fair up to 11.a.m. Misty. Working party near PRONVILLE fired on - 1 horse hit in G.S. Wagon - Hostile fire normal.	
	12th		Observation good - "D" Battery destroyed a G.S. Wagon and team in PRONVILLE - 3 enemy Triplanes seen over BOURLON WOOD - Hostile guns more active than usual - Large explosion seen behind BOIS de BOUCHE.	
	13th		Observation good - Working parties East of PRONVILLE - 3 explosions seen in PRONVILLE - 400 rounds fired during the night.	
	14th		Observation very fair - Assissted in small raid by 3rd WORCESTERS at 10.15.p.m. - Unsuccessful.	
	15th		Heavy rain all day - enemy guns very quiet - Working parties in PRONVILLE fired on.	
	16th		Very wet - Heavy showers all day. between Showers	
	17th		Observation very fair - 81 rounds fired on working parties East of PRONVILLE - Hostile Artillery fire normal - Aircraft inactive.	
	17th		Poor owing to rain - 33 rounds fired on working parties in and about PRONVILLE - Hostile artillery quiet.	
	18th		Observation poor - Hostile artillery rather more active than usual - Section of A/110 heavily shelled midday by 5.9" Battery and again at 4.15.p.m. - No damagex done. 1 F.A. reported to have come down near PRONVILLE.	
	19th		Observation good at intervals - Movement passed SHRINE 1 PRONVILLE fired on - Hostile Artillery normal - Aircraft fairly active on both sides.	
	20th		Observation very fair - Movement near PRONVILLE fired on - Hostile fire normal.	
	21st		Observation good - Working parties fired on S of PRONVILLE - Hostile fire rather above normal - Aircraft not very active.	

Army Form C. 2118.

WAR DIARY
or
INTELLIGENCE SUMMARY. 112th Brigade R.F.A.

(Erase heading not required.)

Instructions regarding War Diaries and Intelligence Summaries are contained in F.S. Regs., Part II. and the Staff Manual respectively. Title pages will be prepared in manuscript.

Place	Date	Hour	Summary of Events and Information	Remarks and references to Appendices
In the Field	Jan 22nd 1918		Observation - fair - Hostile fire normal - Aircraft slight activity.	
	23rd		Observation fair. - 100 rounds fired on movement about PRONVILLE - 150 rounds 5.9" fell in VAULX WOOD. - AIRCRAFT normal.	
	24th		Observation V. fair. - Movement S of PRONVILLE fired at. - Hostile Artillery active E of VAULX - Aircraft normal - "C" Battery moved to new position in 110th area.	
	25th		Observation good. - 80 rounds fired on movement near SHRINE S of PRONVILLE - Hostile artillery fire below normal - E.A. exceedingly active during morning - Our planes V active in afternoon.	
	26th		Observation bad - working party fired on N of PRONVILLE - Enemy guns very quiet - aircraft inactive.	
	27th		Observation bad - TEST S.O.S. at 8.p.m. - 1 round per gun was fired - at 6.45.p.m. few gas shells fell in LAGNICOURT - Aircraft inactive.	
	28th		Observation poor. Hostile Artillery quiet. E.A. active during morning.	
	29th		Observation poor. E.A. bombing machines heard overhead between 9.55.p.m. & 11.45.p.m. Hostile Artillery quiet. D.Battery fired Gas shells on Hostile Battery during night.	
	30th		Observation V. Fair. 50rds fired on movements about PRONVILLE. D.Battery fired 250 rounds on Hostile Battery registered by aeroplane. A patrol of 15 E.A. seen over CURANT at XX 3.30.p.m. comprising 6 Triplanes & 9 Albatross single seaters. Hostile aircraft crossed our lines at midnight to Bomb back areas	
	31st		Very heavy mist obscured all observation, nothing to report.	

Lieut. Col. R.F.A.
Commanding 112th Brigade R.F.A.

Army Form C. 2118.

112 Bn. R.H. Vol 28

WAR DIARY
or
INTELLIGENCE SUMMARY.
(Erase heading not required.)

Place	Date	Hour	Summary of Events and Information	Remarks and references to Appendices
In the Field.	Feb 1st 1918.		Observation very bad.-Thick fog.-Test fired by "A" Battery. 10 secs. Very quiet day.	
	2nd		Observation very fair.-18 pounders fired on movement about PRONVILLE.- "B" & "D" Btys fired Tests 12 secs & 1 min:10secs. 8" How fired about 250 rounds on MARIECOURT WOOD on one of our H.A.Btys.- Hostile Aircraft active during the morning.	
	3rd.		Observation very fair.- "D"Bty fired 158 rounds on Hostile Battery by aeroplane registration. "D" Bty Test 5.36'30" & 5.58'00"P.M. Hostile guns fairly quiet. Movement fired on south of PRONVILLE.- E.A.fairly active.	
	4th.		Observation very fair. Individual movement seen on PRONVILLE-INCHY-RD.- Night Firing. Enemys guns quiet.-Aircraft less inactive.	
	5th		Observation fair- 18 pounders fired on movement -Individual movement seen about PRONVILLE. Slight activty in aircraft.	
	6th		Observation good.-18-pounders assisted Infantry in raid. 1.prisoner & 5 Bosches killed. Hostile guns quiet.-aircraft inactive.	
	7th		Observation fair in the morning poor in the afternoon.-18.pounders fired on movement N.E. PRONVILLE.- Aircraft inactive.	
	8th		Observation fair.-18-Pounders fired on movement.-Movement above normal night-firing for "A"&"B" Batteries -Aircraft inactive.- Hostile guns quiet.	
	9th		Observation very good.-Movement fired on.-Night Harassing fire carried out.Hostile guns very active."D"Bty was shelled during day by 5'9 & 4'2 from BOISDE BOCCHE. 1.pit damaged. Aircraft inactive.	
	10th		Observation good. Great deal of movement seen in trenches & roads leading to QUEANT& PRONVILLE: Shelled by 18-pounders.	

Army Form C. 2118.

WAR DIARY
or
INTELLIGENCE SUMMARY.
(Erase heading not required.)

Instructions regarding War Diaries and Intelligence Summaries are contained in F. S. Regs., Part II. and the Staff Manual respectively. Title pages will be prepared in manuscript.

Place	Date	Hour	Summary of Events and Information	Remarks and references to Appendices
In the Field.	10th		Continued. Hostile guns shelled our trenches in the afternoon and from 10 to 11p.m. -Our guns retaliated on Birdcage.- E.A. inactive.- Our planes fairly active.	
	11th		Observation good.- 18-pounders fired on movements in vicinity of PRONVILLE. some casualties caused. Hostile guns very active XXXXX "C"Bty old position shot up. a few shells falling into "B" Bty forward section.- Enemys guns were also very active at night shooting on CRUCIFIX N.W of MORCHIES.& LEECH AVENUE.)Our guns retaliated at 12.15.a.m.- E.A. inactive. Slight activity on our side.	
	12th.		Observation fair-misty. 18-pounders fired on movement North of PRONVILLE & 60 rounds at 9.5.p.m. on BOISSY)PRONVILLE RD.in retaliation to hostile fire on our trenches . Enemys guns less active than two previous days. aircraft inactive.	
	13th		Observation poor.rain. 1 sect"A" relieved by 1 sect 42nd Bty. 1 sect "D" relieved by 1 sect 87th Bty during night.	
	14th		All Battery W.L. moved to MEAULTE at 9.a.m. Gun line personnel & H.Q. left W.L. by Moter Lorry at 8.p.m.	
	15th		General cleaning up & drawing guns from 110th Brigade in new area.	
	16th		General cleaning up & Training carried out in new area.	
	17th		-do-	
	18th		-do-	
	19th		-do-	
	20th		-do-	
	21st		-do-	

Army Form C. 2118.

WAR DIARY
or
INTELLIGENCE SUMMARY.
(Erase heading not required.)

Instructions regarding War Diaries and Intelligence Summaries are contained in F. S. Regs., Part II. and the Staff Manual respectively. Title pages will be prepared in manuscript.

Place	Date	Hour	Summary of Events and Information	Remarks and references to Appendices
In the Field.	22nd		General cleaning up & Training carried out in new area.	
	23rd.		General cleaning up & Training carried out in new area.	
	24th		General cleaning up & Training carried out in new area.	
	25th		General cleaning up & Training carried out in new area.	
	26th		"C" Bty Calibrated guns drawn from Gun Park ALBERT on range at FRICOURT. "A" BTy. moved to vicinity of FREMICOURT and attached to 51st D.A.	
	27th		"D" Bty Calibrated their Hows on range at FRICOURT.-Preparations made by B.H.Q. & "C" & "D" Btys for move to new area. BOCQUOY.	
	28th		Brigade Headquarters and "C" & "D" Batteries moved to new area.	
	28.2.18			

signature Lieut.Col. ?????, R.F.A.

Commanding 112th Brigade R.F.A.

25th Divisional Artillery.

WAR DIARY

112th BRIGADE

ROYAL FIELD ARTILLERY

MARCH 1 9 1 8

Army Form C. 2118.

WAR DIARY
or
INTELLIGENCE SUMMARY

(Erase heading not required.) of 112th. Brigade R.F.A.

MARCH 1918

Place	Date	Hour	Summary of Events and Information	Remarks and references to Appendices
In the March Fields	1st.		General cleaning.	
"	2nd.		Training as per programme shown.	
"	3rd.		Baths and Training, Wet day.	
"	4th.		Training as per programme.	
"	5th.		do.	
"	6th.		do.	
"	7th.		C.R.A. Conference at Divl. Arty. Fine day. Training and General Duties carried out near BUCQUOY.	
"	8th.		do.	
"	9th.		do.	
"	10th.		do.	
"	11th.		do.	
"	12th.		do.	
"	13th.		do.	
"	14th.		do.	
"	15th.		do.	
"	16th.		do.	
"	17th.		do.	

Instructions regarding War Diaries and Intelligence Summaries are contained in F. S. Regs., Part II. and the Staff Manual respectively. Title Pages will be prepared in manuscript.

2449 Wt. W14957/M90 750,000 1/16 J.B.C. & A. Forms/C.2118/12.

Army Form C. 2118.

WAR DIARY
or
INTELLIGENCE SUMMARY

(Erase heading not required.) of 112th. Brigade R.F.A.   MARCH 1918   II (continued)

Instructions regarding War Diaries and Intelligence Summaries are contained in F.S. Regs., Part II. and the Staff Manual respectively. Title Pages will be prepared in manuscript.

Place	Date	Hour	Summary of Events and Information	Remarks and references to Appendices
In the Field	March 18th.		Training and General Duties carried out near BUCQUOY.	
"	19th.		do. do.	
"	20th.		do. do.	
"	21st.		Hd.Qrs., B & D. Batteries moved to A/112 Wagon Line at 9.am. from BUCQUOY. Batteries went into action near Butts 800 yards East of BEUGNY. AA & C wagon lines heavily shelled during morning. C. 14 Casualties. A. 4. Hd. Qrs. in sunken road East of MORCHIES. These Hd.Qrs. were evacuated at 2.am. when Hd.Qrs. returned to Butts.	
"	22nd.		Bde. Withdrew to positions near Cemetery East of BANCOURT. Many horses killed, about 20 casualties to personnel were caused during retirement. D. Battery did not retire until about 2.am. on 22nd. 2nd.Lt. Swann wounded Hd.Qrs. at FREMICOURT.	
"	23rd.		Bde. Withdrew from positions near Cemetery at 5.pm. to positions between BANCOURT and BIENCOURT. Hd.Qrs. on left Flank of Batteries, 2nd.Lt. Gordon wounded. Batteries heavily shelled during day. B. Battery had two guns knocked out and A. Battery 1. Bde Signal Officer wounded. Major Swinton wounded.	
"	24th.		Bde. retired at 5.pm. to take up positions west of THILLOY. Orders were then received to move to GREVILLERS. On arriving there Bde again received orders to move to positions of Assembly West of ACHIET-le-PETIT.	
"	25th.		Batteries moved to positions S.W. of MIRAUMONT at 5.am. Bde. retired to ROSSIGNOL WOOD in the evening with the exception of one gun of D. Battery which continued to cover the Infantry withdrawing at night. Orders for a further retirement to FONQUEVILLERS, which should have reached the Bde. at ROSSIGNOL WOOD did not arrive, so that the Bde. A and B. Batteries did not retire until all the Infantry had gone. C and D Batteries were attached to 104 Bde. and left ROSSIGNOL WOOD at 8.pm.	
"	26th.		Hd.Qrs. with A and C Batteries retired at 5. am. to positions on road 500 yards south of FONQUEVILLERS. Shortly after coming into position, enemy were reported to be coming through HEBUTERNE. Great confusion on road through 60 pdrs. attempting to withdraw their guns. Batteries withdrew there thier guns about 400 yards with the exception of B and D. Batteries. Enemy attacked but were repulsed in the evening Bde. Hdrs. with C Battery.	
"	27th.		Bde. Hd.Qrs. moved to gun pits near CHair de – la HAIE. Australians relieved the 19th. Division. Adjutant rejoined Bde, from Divl. Arty.	

Army Form C. 2118.

MARCH 1918.

WAR DIARY
or
INTELLIGENCE SUMMARY

(Erase heading not required.) of 112th. Brigade. R.F.A. (continued)

Instructions regarding War Diaries and Intelligence Summaries are contained in F. S. Regs., Part II. and the Staff Manual respectively. Title Pages will be prepared in manuscript.

Place	Date	Hour	Summary of Events and Information	Remarks and references to Appendices
In the Field	March. 28th.		Bde. moved to positions north of MAILLY - MAILLET, under orders of 4th. N.Z. Div. Arty. Hd.Qrs. under Railway right flank of A. Battery GROUPED with 110th. Bde.	
"	29th.		General Registration.	
"	30th.		Situation Normal. Wet day. MAILLY - MAILLET shelled.	
"	31st.		O.P. selected by O.C. Bde. in the front line. Night harrassing fire.	

Malcolm Capt. R.A. for
Lieut. Col.
Commanding 112th. Bde. R.F.A.

25th Divisional Artillery

WAR DIARY

112th BRIGADE

ROYAL FIELD ARTILLERY

APRIL 1918

Army Form C. 2118.

WAR DIARY
or
INTELLIGENCE-SUMMARY.   112th Brigade R.F.A.

(Erase heading not required.)

Instructions regarding War Diaries and Intelligence Summaries are contained in F. S. Regs., Part II. and the Staff Manual respectively. Title pages will be prepared in manuscript.

Place	Date	Hour	Summary of Events and Information	Remarks and references to Appendices
In The Field	April 1st 1918		Batteries still in action between MAILLY - MAILLET and COLINCAMPS. Wagon Lines just W of BERTRANCOURT. An uneventful day except for intermittent shelling by enemy of villages and back areas. 800 rounds 18 pounder and 200 rounds 4.5" fired in night harassing fire. Captain S.O. Jones appointed Major of A/112 vice Major Swinton, wounded - Lieut A.C.R. DAVID appointed Captain of A/112 vice Jones promoted.	
	2nd.		Enemy activity confined to shelling of back areas and villages - S.O.S. barrage lines continually being altered owing to Infantry forming Advanced posts ; 2 Batteries manned Front line O.Ps daily and one at night and a Liaison Officer with Right Battalion Left Divn. 600 rounds Night Harrassing fire.	
	3rd.		At 2.30.a.m. a Thorough gas bombardment by 3. 4.5" How Batteries assisted by 18 pounders was carried out on 3 suspected hostile Inf.H.Qrs. 1800 rounds R.N.C. were fired. The bosch was quiet except for his usual back area shoots. Night firing was carried out as usual.	
	4th		At 9.p.m. the 1st (centre) N.Z. Brigade withdrew from line and 3rd N.R.B. (left) took over their front and handed over the part North of RED COTTAGE to Div on North ; 112th Brigade then covered Right and centre Battalions of Left Brigade. - Night firing as usual.	
	5th		At 5.30.a.m. the Left group assisted 37th Divn in an attack - D Btty put up a smoke barrage firing 1000 rounds and the 18 pounders bombarded trenches commanding the scene of operations. At 7.30.a.m. enemy opened very heavy barrage on trenches and all back areas and battery areas. He attacked without success. Our casualties were 3 killed and 3 wounded which were astoundingly light considering the extreme violence of enemy artillery during whole morning and at intervals during afternoon - A counter preparation was fired from 7.30.p.m. to 7.54.p.m. and 1000 rounds 18 pounder and 200 rounds how in night firing - Enemy Artillery during night was not heavy.	
	6th		A full counter preparation was fired from 5.a.m. to 5.45.a.m. in anticipation of renewed enemy efforts, Hostile Artillery was very quiet until about 11.a.m. when odd bursts of fire was started on tracks and back areas.	
	7th		Marched to SARTON at 8.30.a.m. having been relieved by 293 Bde R.F.A.	
	8th		Remained at SARTON for the day - Very wet.	

Army Form C. 2118.

WAR DIARY
or
INTELLIGENCE SUMMARY. 112th Brigade R.F.A.

(Erase heading not required.)

Instructions regarding War Diaries and Intelligence Summaries are contained in F. S. Regs, Part II. and the Staff Manual respectively. Title pages will be prepared in manuscript.

Place	Date	Hour	Summary of Events and Information	Remarks and references to Appendices
In the Field.	April 9th 1918		Brigade marched to HERNICOURT.	
	10th		Brigade marched to COTTES.	
	11th		Brigade marched to MORBECQUE.	
	12th		Brigade marched into action near ST HANS CAPPELL.	
	13th		"C" Battery had 2 killed and 1 wounded - 2nd Lieut Goodman wounded - Enemy attacked with 2 Divisions about 4.30.p.m. until late in the evening, but was repulsed. "D" battery had 2 men wounded.	
	14th		Enemy attacked from 6.a.m. to about 11.a.m., but was repulsed - 2nd Lieut H.S. GORDON wounded at O.P. believed serious. Enemy put down a heavy barrage on our trenches South of METEREN at 4.5.p.m.	
	15th		Brigade moved at 11.p.m. to rear positions "A" and "C" just West of MONT DES CATS - "B" and "D" on the BERTHEN - MONT DES CATS Road.	
	16th		B.H.Q. moved from BERTHEN AREA to Farm on West slope of MONT DES CATS. at 3.p.m.	
	17th		Enemy attacked our front South of METEREN at 9.30.a.m. - attack lasted until 12 noon without any success. During the attack enemy shelled back areas and batteries very heavily. "A" and "C" Batteries had 5 killed and 24 wounded including 2 Lieut N. GOOCH and 2nd Lieut GODEMAN (Wounded) 25 horses were killed. Enemy shelled GODEWAERSVELDE with 12 inch gun, base of shell was found. "A" Battery moved forward about 1000 yards at 5.p.m.	
	18th		"C" Battery moved forward early morning about 600 yards in to new position.	
	19th		Quiet day - Snowed.	

Army Form C. 2118.

WAR DIARY
or
INTELLIGENCE SUMMARY.   112th Brigade R.F.A.

(Erase heading not required.)

Instructions regarding War Diaries and Intelligence Summaries are contained in F. S. Regs., Part II. and the Staff Manual respectively. Title pages will be prepared in manuscript.

Place	Date	Hour	Summary of Events and Information	Remarks and references to Appendices
In The Field.	20th April 1918		Brigade moved to new positions north of the FLETRE - CAESTRE road. Move commenced at 7.a.m. Harassing fire carried out during the night 20/21st - Counter preparation between 4 and 5 a.m. Brigade covers 3rd Australian Inf Bde.	
	21st.		Fine day - Two enemy Batteries seen firing - Counter preparation carried out 4.30.a.m. to 5.30.a.m.	
	22nd.		"C" Battery M.G. claims to have brought down enemy plane which was flying very low over our lines.	
	23rd.		"A" Battery had 1 man wounded by bomb dropped by low flying plane - while laying wires. - EECKE shelled during the night. - Hostile bombing planes active during the day.	
	24th		Heavy firing to Right and Left of Brigade Zone during the night - Counter preparation in the morning at 4.a.m. - Hostile bombing planes active at night.	
	25th		Enemy long range guns active on back areas all day - O.C. reconnoitred reserve positions west of CAESTRE. "C" Battery mess shelled at intervals by 5.9" during the evening. Several direct hits on officers quarters - 1 man wounded. 25th D.A. take over from 33rd D.A. - 1 E.A. flew very low over Battery positions at 1.15.p.m. - 8 O.Rs of "B" Battery suffering from burns caused by direct hit on barn with a mustard gas shell.	
	26th		"C" Battery were shot up by 4.2" and 5.9" in the evening - no damage was done to the guns, but Officers quarters destroyed. Two or three 8" fell between guns and mess.	
	27th		Fairly quiet day.	
	28th		Heavy barrage heard N.E. of BAILLEUL about 6.30.p.m. continuing off and on all night.	
	29th		Barrage N. of BAILLEUL increased at its highest about 10.30.a.m. SCHERPENBERG reported lost. Counter preparation carried out mid-day. Several hostile batteries seen firing near OUTTERSTEENE engaged by 18 pounders - Enemy attack driven off ; We still hold SCHERPENBERG 25th Div attacked 4 times.	

Army Form C. 2118.

WAR DIARY
or
INTELLIGENCE SUMMARY.   112th Brigade R.F.A.
(Erase heading not required.)

Instructions regarding War Diaries and Intelligence Summaries are contained in F. S. Regs., Part II. and the Staff Manual respectively. Title pages will be prepared in manuscript.

Place	Date	Hour	Summary of Events and Information	Remarks and references to Appendices
In the Field	April 30th 1918.		Quiet day - Barrage lasting about half an hour heard about 8.p.m. in direction of BAILLEUL. 112th, 110th, and 113th Bdes fired 6 rounds gun fire on a 4.2" Battery which had moved very much forward, at 12 noon.	

R. Mann.
Lieut. Col: R.F.A.
Adjutant 112th Brigade R.F.A.

Army Form C. 2118.

WAR DIARY
or
INTELLIGENCE SUMMARY.

112th Brigade R.F.A.

(Erase heading not required.)

Instructions regarding War Diaries and Intelligence Summaries are contained in F.S. Regs., Part II. and the Staff Manual respectively. Title pages will be prepared in manuscript.

Place	Date	Hour	Summary of Events and Information	Remarks and references to Appendices
In the Field.	May 1st 1918		Brigade in action North of METEREN.	
	2nd.		Quiet Day.	
	3rd.		METEREN and CAESTRE shelled by 7.7.mm during morning.	
	4th.		Area shoot by 4.2" in neighbourhood of "C" and "B" Batteries.	
	5th.		Quiet day - Nothing to report.	
	6th.		1 Section per Battery relieved by 30th Divl. Artillery.	
	7th.		Remainder relieved. - Marched to LYNDE.	
	8th.		Cleaning up.	
	9th		1.a.m. 4 heavy bombs dropped beside B.H.Q. - about 35 casualties caused.	
	9th.		Cleaning up and preparing for entraining.	
	10th.		Brigade entrained at WIZERNES and ARQUES in the morning.	
	11th.		Batteries arrived in the evening - detraining at FISMES and SAVIGNY and marched to BROUILLET.	
	12th.		Cleaning up and general fatigues.	
	13th.		Brigade training commenced.	
	14th.		Brigade training.	
	15th to 23rd.		Brigade training continued - Occasional Football matches	

Army Form C. 2118.

WAR DIARY
or
INTELLIGENCE-SUMMARY.   112th Brigade R.F.A.

(Erase heading not required.)

Instructions regarding War Diaries and Intelligence Summaries are contained in F.S. Regs., Part II. and the Staff Manual respectively. Title pages will be prepared in manuscript.

Place	Date	Hour	Summary of Events and Information	Remarks and references to Appendices
In the Field.	24th May 1918		Brigade marched to BAISLIEUX.	
	25th		Final of Inter-Battery Football competition - "B" Battery beating "D" Battery.	
	26th		Brigade marched into action leaving BASLIEUX at 7.30.p.m.	
	27th		Batteries and B.H.Q. arrived at their position S.W. of CORMICY at 1.a.m. just as the preliminary bombardment commenced. - Many horses were killed on the road leading to positions and consequently road was blocked for 2 hours - "C" Battery was unable to get into action until 3.30.a.m. a Large proportion of shells were BLUE CROSS. Battery positions were heavily shelled from 1.a.m. to 12 noon. - 21st Divl. Arty retired covered by 112th Brigade at 1.p.m. - At 5.p.m. considerable rifle anf machine gun fire was heard on our left rear bullets coming over B.H.Q. 7.10.p.m. patrol sent out by Headquarters reported enemy in our rear and working through the wood about 200 yards away. - Enemy placed a machine gun on road running from Headquarters to Battery positions which prevented any of the horses of Brigade Headquarters reaching us and all wagons had to be left. - "C" Battery being the nearest to H.Qrs were also unable to bring their horses up and finally after holding up the enemy for 2 hours were compelled to abandon their guns after blowing them up. - Colonel SARSON was successful in collecting sufficient Infantry who were retiring through the guns to hold up the enemies advance for two hours in the hope that "C" Battery teams might arrive. Colonel SRASON finally ordered the guns to be destroyed - He then retired with 2nd Lieut A.O. STANDEN and several Other Ranks, but on entering BOUVANCOURT about 9.30.p.m. was taken prisoner together with 2nd Lieut A.O. STANDEN who were leading the party, as the enemy were then holding the village - The remainder of the party about 6 men who were some distance behind the Colonel managed to get away.	
	28th.		Brigade came under the Orders of Colonel PHIPPS, D.S.O.- "A" and "C" Batteries marched to VANDEUL arriving at 5.a.m. - "B" Battery and B.H.Q. marched to SAVIGNY arriving at 6.a.m. "D" Battery came into action near VANDEUL later in the day. "A" - "B" - "D" Batteries came into action near SAVIGNY firing on VANDEUL. B.H.Q. and "C" Battery moved back to AUGNY moving again at 11.p.m. to VILLERS ARGON.	

Army Form C. 2118.

WAR DIARY
or
INTELLIGENCE-SUMMARY. 112th Brigade R.F.A.

(Erase heading not required.)

Instructions regarding War Diaries and Intelligence Summaries are contained in F. S. Regs., Part II. and the Staff Manual respectively. Title pages will be prepared in manuscript.

Place	Date	Hour	Summary of Events and Information	Remarks and references to Appendices
In The Field.	May 29th 1917		"A" "B" and "D" Batteries moved during the night of 28th/29th to position EAST of BROUILLET.	
	30th		"D" Battery moved to position N.W. of VILLE -en - TARDENOIS - "A" and "B" Batteries moved back to positions S of LHERY - B.H.Q. and "C" Battery moved to LA CHAPELLE. "D" Battery moved to NANTEUIL for the night 30th/31st. "A" and "B" Batteries took up positions S edge of BOIS des ECLISSES.	
	31st		"D" Battery moved up to position East of VILLE en TARDENOIS from which position they knocked out 2 hostile guns.	

J H H ____ Lt Col
Major R.F.A.
Commanding 112th Brigade R.F.A.

Army Form C. 2118.

WAR DIARY
or
INTELLIGENCE SUMMARY. 112th Brigade R.F.A.
(Erase heading not required.)

Place	Date	Hour	Summary of Events and Information	Remarks and references to Appendices
In The Field.	June 1st 1918		B.H.Q. and C/112 marched to COLLIGNY from ORBAIS. - A/112 were in action S Edge of BOIS des ECLISSES with B/112. - D/112 in action beside CHAUMUZY.	
	2nd.		"A" and "B" Batteries moved to positions just west of BOIS D'AULNAY - D/112 moved into North edge of BOIS D'AULNAY.	
	3rd.		B.H.Q. relieved H.Q. of 45th Brigade less Col. BALLARD who took over group - C/112 relieved composite battery 110th Brigade R.F.A.	
	4th.		Enemy attacked at 3.10.a.m. on our front and took MONT de BLIGNY which was re-taken by the troops on our right at 6.30.p.m. - B.H.Q. moved with H.Q. 7th I.B. to N.E. corner of BOIS de COURTON.	
	5th.		Quiet Day.	
	6th.		Quiet day - A/110 relieved B/112 who marched to their rear W.Ls.	
	7th.		Quiet day. B/112 marched to COLLIGNY - 2nd Lieut F.G. BENT wounded.	
	8th.		Very quiet - 2nd Lieut C.F. BUTLER was wounded and died of wounds. -	
	9th.		Nothing to report - quiet.	
	10th.		Very quiet on our front.	
	11th.		Very quiet on our front - Night firing carried out.	
	12th		Usual day and night firing carried out. - Quiet on our Front.	
	13th		Night firing and Area shoots carried out. - Quiet day.	
	14th		Usual firing carried out -	

Army Form C. 2118.

WAR DIARY
or
INTELLIGENCE-SUMMARY. 112th Brigade R.F.A.

(Erase heading not required.)

Instructions regarding War Diaries and Intelligence Summaries are contained in F.S. Regs., Part II. and the Staff Manual respectively. Title pages will be prepared in manuscript.

Place	Date	Hour	Summary of Events and Information	Remarks and references to Appendices
In the Field	June 15th 1918		During early morning 1 section from A/112, A/110, C/112 withdrew to new positions just East of BOIS D'AULNAY.	
	16th		Remaining guns of A/112 A/110 and C/112 moved into new positions.	
	17th		During night 1 section of each Battery was relieved by Italian Batteries, but our positions were not taken over, fresh ones some 800 yards in rear being selected.	
	18th		Remaining sections relieved marching to Forward W..s near HAUTVILLERS - B.H.Q. relieved by 1st ITALIAN GROUP.	
	19th		Brigade remained in Forward W.Ls - Billeting parties from Batteries sent forward to VERTUS.	
	20th		Brigade marched to VERTUS at 2.a.m.	
	21st		Brigade marched to OGNES joining 110th Brigade and B/112.	
	22nd		Cleaning up.	
	23rd		Cleaning up. 110th Brigade left to entrain at ARCIS -sur - AUBE.	
	24th		112th Brigade marched to SOMMESOUS - "A" Battery with 2. G.S. wagons and teams and 4 limbered wagons and teams of No 2 Section D.A.C. left SOMMESOUS by train at 11.30.p.m.	
	25th		"B" Battery with portion of D.A.C. left by train at 5.30.a.m. "C" Battery Left at 7.50.a.m. "D" Battery left at 11.30.a.m. B.H.Q. with H.Q. No.2 Section D.A.C. left by train at 3.30.p.m.	
	26th		In Train.	
	27th		Brigade detrained :- B.H.Q. at HESDIN. - "A" Battery at HESDIN. - "B" Battery at MARESQUEL- "C" Battery at ANVIN. - "D" Battery at HESDIN. B.H.Q. and Batteries marched to HUMBERT.	

Army Form C. 2118.

WAR DIARY
or
INTELLIGENCE-SUMMARY. ~~Xxx~~ 112th Brigade R.F.A.

(Erase heading not required.)

Place	Date	Hour	Summary of Events and Information	Remarks and references to Appendices
In The Field.	28th June 1918		General cleaning up - 3 day fever breaks out in "D" Battery.	
	29th		General cleaning up. - "A" Battery drew 1 gun and "B" Battery 6 making the Brigade complete.	
	30th		Brigade marched to VEIL- HESDIN at 8.a.m. arriving at 4.p.m.	

[signature]

Lieut. Col. R.F.A.
Commanding 112th Brigade R.F.A.

Army Form C. 2118.

WAR DIARY
or
INTELLIGENCE SUMMARY

112th Brigade R.F.A.

(Erase heading not required.)

Vol 33

Place	Date	Hour	Summary of Events and Information	Remarks and references to Appendices
In the Field.	July. 1st 1918		Brigade marched from VIEIL HESDIN to HEM arriving 12.45 pm. 3 day fever appears for first time in "C" Battery.	
	2nd.		General cleaning up.	
	3rd		General fatigues.	
	4th		General fatigues.	
	5th		Adjutant and 1 Officer per Battery went up by lorry to see N.Z. Div Arty at GOUIN.	
	6th.		Orders to move the following day received.	
	7th.		Brigade marched at 7.30 am. to COUIN arriving in Wagon lines about 12 noon. 82 L.D & 2 R.1 Remounts drawn a good lot.	
	8th.		1 Section detailed from C/112 as mobile anti-Tank section went up to XXXX Chateau de la HAIE in the evening.	
	9th.		Balloon brought down by E.A. near COUIN. E.A. is reported to have been shot down in our lines on its return.	
	10th.		"A" Battery marched to FROHEN-le-GRAND to calibrate guns. B/112 had a section standing by as mobile anti-tank section for B/110. Section from B/110 relieved mobile anti-tank section of C/112 in the evening about 9.30 pm. Two sections from C/112 marched to FROHEN-le-GRAND about 6.pm.	
	11th		Remaining section of C/112 and B/112 marched to FROHEN-le-GRAND at 6 am. to calibrate A/112 marched from FROHEN-le-GRAND to wagon lines at COUIN.	
	12th		B & C Batteries returned to COUIN. Mobile anti-tank section from C/112 relieved section from B/110 in the evening.	

Army Form C. 2118.

WAR DIARY
or
INTELLIGENCE SUMMARY.   112th Brigade R.F.A.

(Erase heading not required.)

Instructions regarding War Diaries and Intelligence Summaries are contained in F. S. Regs., Part II. and the Staff Manual respectively. Title pages will be prepared in manuscript.

Place	Date	Hour	Summary of Events and Information	Remarks and references to Appendices
In the field.	July 13th 1918.		D.Battery marched to FROHEN-le-GRAND at 5.45.a.m.	
	14th.		D.Battery returned to Wagon lines at GOUIN. 3.H.V.shells fell in AUTHIE about midnight.	
	15th.		Brigade Training carried out.	
	16th		Brigade Training carried out.	
	17th.		About 2 am. 8 bombs fell near AUTHIE.	
	18th		Corps Artillery Test 112th allotted to 37th D.A.	
	19th		Brigade Training carried out.	
	20th		Inspection by General Geddes G.O.C.,R.A., IV Corps.	
	21st		Brigade Training carried out.	
	22nd		Lt. Col. Queripel C.M.G.,D.S.O. Lectured to N.C.O.s class.	
	23rd		Brigade Training continued.	
	24th		Usual Brigade Training carried out.	
	25th to 27th		Brigade training carried out at GOUIN. Received orders to relieve Brigade of 57th D.A., but these were cancelled.	
	28th		Received orders that Divl Artillery was transferred to III Corps and marched from GOUIN to CONTAY leaving the starting point at ST LEGER at 11.30.p.m.	
	29th		Brigade at CONTAY.	

Army Form C. 2118.

WAR DIARY
or
INTELLIGENCE SUMMARY.

112th Brigade R.F.A.

(Erase heading not required.)

Instructions regarding War Diaries and Intelligence Summaries are contained in F. S. Regs., Part II. and the Staff Manual respectively. Title pages will be prepared in manuscript.

Place	Date	Hour	Summary of Events and Information	Remarks and references to Appendices
In The Field.	July 30th 1918		The Brigade still at CONTAY. About 6.40.p.m. 9 shells were fired by the enemy into CONTAY - 1 horse killed and 2 wounded.	
	31st		1 Section of Batteries relieved section of Batteries of the 58th D.A.	

J.H.Queripel Lieut. Col. R.F.A.
Commanding 112th Brigade R.F.A.

WAR DIARY
or
INTELLIGENCE SUMMARY.

112th Brigade R.F.A. Army Form C. 2118.

Vol 34

Place	Date	Hour	Summary of Events and Information	Remarks and references to Appendices
In the Field	Aug 1st 1918		B.H.Q. went into the line to take over the Hd Qrs from the 29th Bde. 58th Bde. Renewing destores relieved renewing section 291 Bde.	
	2nd		Reputation carried out. Night firing	
	3rd		Very quiet in the line. Nothing further to report.	
	4th		- do - - do -	
	5th		- do - - do -	
	6th		- do - - do -	
	7th		Sgt. Major Stokes killed whilst taking up ammunition to A. Bty. A drone's double planes attacked German line station to Brulsfort 10 a.m.	
	8th		Attack commenced 4.20am. Went successful. Whole fg: unlimb 12 am. Very good shooting carried out by B/112 on Parties of the enemy in the open. MORLANCOURT captured in the afternoon. Enemy barrage very slight. B. Bty moved up to the right H-A. Bty getting into action. On casualties 3 officers 12 O.R.	

Army Form C. 2118.

WAR DIARY
or
INTELLIGENCE SUMMARY.
(Erase heading not required.)

112th Bde R.F.A.

Place	Date	Hour	Summary of Events and Information	Remarks and references to Appendices
In the Field	Aug 9th 1918		We attacked at 5.30 P.M. Except for one small portion of trench and a Ry cutting all objectives were gained. (S.J. MEAULT) Hostile barrage was not heavy very few guns appeared to be firing until planes bombed back areas.	
"	10th		We attacked at 6 P.M. and took the Ry Cutting and trench - again which we were unable to take the day before. Orders for this attack were not received until 5.45 P.M. A/112 did some excellent shooting on Parties of the enemy in the open, firing altogether about 800 rounds. Enemys planes bombed villages in forward areas between 10 P.M. + midnight.	
"	11th		Enemy put down a heavy barrage in the early front at 4.15 am. Our Batteries fired a few bursts in their S.O.S. lines. B.#.B. moved to 40m previously occupied by 169 Bde. D/232 reporting to Brigade.	
"	12th		Quiet day. B. #. B. moved to 40m previously occupied by 169 Bde. D/232 reporting to Brigade. at 3.30 am. 3.45 am about 50 x do - 4.2. fell in valley between B + D Bdys. Light harassing fire was carried out by all Batteries.	
"	13th		At 4.55am local attack commenced on some high ground about 200 yards due South of MEAULT. This was captured and posts established on the Eastern slopes. Visibility was bad. Enemy shelled EMU trench at 6.15 am with H.E. + G.	

Army Form C. 2118.

112th Bde R.F.A

WAR DIARY
or
INTELLIGENCE SUMMARY.
(Erase heading not required.)

Instructions regarding War Diaries and Intelligence Summaries are contained in F. S. Regs., Part II. and the Staff Manual respectively. Title pages will be prepared in manuscript.

Place	Date	Hour	Summary of Events and Information	Remarks and references to Appendices
In the Field	Aug 13th 1918		5 9s, 4.2" shelled area near Battery O.Ps with intermittently throughout the day. Night firing carried out by the Bde on Roads and Approaches.	
	14th		During the morning 8/12 silenced an A.A Bty which was worrying our planes. 4.2" Bty shelled area round about Bty O.P. intermittently during the morning. About 20 gas shell fell near B. Bty at 4 a.m.	
	15th		Visibility poor. Hostile guns quiet. Slight shelling of DERNACOURT by 4.2° during the day. Night harassing fire carried out by 18 Pdrs & 4.5 hows.	
	16th		Visibility poor. Hostile guns rather more active than usual shelling trenches in the vicinity of our O.Ps. C. Bty fired 150 Rds on movement SE of ALBERT. E.A. machine gun between 3 & 5 Pm about 70 ft fell in valley	
	17th		Visibility very fair. A. C. Bty and B. Bty. Considerable movement observed on FRICOURT & BECORDEL Rd mainly M.T. proceeding both ways, also often martin eyelash seen fired on Bty 18 Pdrs & 4.A. Night harassing fire 18 Pdrs fired 650 rounds & 4.5 hows 120 rounds.	

Army Form C. 2118.

WAR DIARY
or
INTELLIGENCE SUMMARY.
(Erase heading not required.)

112th Bde R.F.A

Place	Date	Hour	Summary of Events and Information	Remarks and references to Appendices
In the Field	Aug 18th 1918		Visibility good. Considerable movement seen on FRICOURT - BECORDEL Rd mainly M.T. proceeding West. Fire on Inf 18 Pdrs. and #7 Hostile Artillery fairly active in valley between C.Bdy & 13 Bdy 130 about 150 rounds 5.9 = 4.2 Falling there during the day. Night harassing fire by 18 Pdrs +4.5 How Complin preparation carried out by Bde from 4.15 am to 4.45 am	
"	19th		Visibility very fair. Considerable movement on FRICOURT BECORDEL Rd M.T. going west. Fired on Inf 18 Pdrs. A few men seen proceeding Eastward on same road. Hostile guns less active than usual. No night harassing fire was carried out	
	20th		Quiet day. Movement near BECORDEL fired on Inf 18 Pdrs. Night Harassing fire carried out.	
	21st		Bde opened fire at 4.45 am for attack on trenches S. of MEAULT. Successful operation. very slight resistance. Ar.B. Bdes moved up to position west of Rly East of MEAULT. at 6.30 am	
	22nd		Bde opened fire at 4.45am for attack on MEAULT entirely successful.	

Army Form C. 2118.

WAR DIARY
or
INTELLIGENCE SUMMARY.   112th Bde R.F.A.
(Erase heading not required.)

Place	Date	Hour	Summary of Events and Information	Remarks and references to Appendices
In the Field	Aug 23rd 1918		Quiet day. Bde moved forward about 1000 yards during the night.	
	24th		Batteries moved at 8 a.m. to positions just east of MEAULT. B.H.Q. moved to dug out about 1500 yards S of the village.	
	25th		Bde attacked BECORDEL at 2.30am. Successful operation.	
	26th		B.H.Q. moved to Hidden Wood East of FRICOURT at 6 a.m. with 3s Inf Bde. Batteries in action S. of MAMETZ. Attack on High ground East of CARNOY at 4 am. Final objective was not taken.	
	27th		Attacked High ground East of CARNOY at 4.55 am and reached line west of FAYIERE Wood and high ground to the north. Division attacked at 4.55am & took HARDECOURT. Batteries moved forward at 9. at 3/4 hour interval in action Aug 12.15 am north of MARICOURT. B.H.Q. moved from HIDDEN WOOD to # Bd 500 yards	
	28th		north of CARNOY.	

Army Form C. 2118.

WAR DIARY
or
INTELLIGENCE SUMMARY.   112th Bde R.F.A

(Erase heading not required.)

Place	Date	Hour	Summary of Events and Information	Remarks and references to Appendices
In the Field	Aug 29th 1918		1 Section from A.B.C. Batteries went forward with Cavalry under Major McKay and came into action about 500 yds s.E. of MAUREPAS. At one time they came into action 500 yds East of our outpost line and did a considerable amount of damage.	
	30th		Bde H.Qrs moved up at 7. a.m. to Hd Qrs just West of MAUREPAS near Advanced Personnel Report Centre and received orders for the Bde to move up to Advanced Positions. Batteries South of LE FOREST Battries in action by 1 P.m. Wagon Lines moved to CURLU in the afternoon. Bde is now affiliated to 141 Inf Bde 47th Division. They having taken over from the 38th Bde 12th Division	
	31st		Bde turned in at 5. 30am to attack on LEG of MUTTON WOOD and High Ground to the East of it. Operations very successful. About 70 prisoners being taken and 2 of our men who were taken prisoners on March 28 escaped to our lines.	

L.H.Quirpel Lt. Col
Commanding 112th Bde R.F.A

31-8-18

WAR DIARY or INTELLIGENCE-SUMMARY.

112th Bde R.F.A.

Army Form C. 2118.

(Erase heading not required.)

Place	Date	Hour	Summary of Events and Information	Remarks and references to Appendices
In the Field.	1st Sept 1918		attacked at 5.30.a.m. and reached final objective - line of trenches running along S.W. edge of ST PIERRE VAAST WOOD. Considerable number of prisoners taken - 58th Div gained their objective on our right. Batteries moved to forward positions about 2000^x S of RANCOURT at 5.15.p.m. B.H.Q. did not move.	
	2nd.		Barrage opened at 5.30.a.m. for attack on ST PIERRE VAAST WOOD.	
	3rd.		D/112 fired 120 gas shell into VAUX WOOD. Took over duties with 142nd Inf Bde from 62nd Bde R.F.A. 2 enemy balloons brought down - B.H.Q. Move to LE FOREST.	
	4th.		MOISLAINS very heavily shelled. - B.H.Q. Moved to NEEDLE WOOD. - "A" and "B" Batteries moved forward to positions W. of MOISLAINS.	
	5th.		B.H.Q. moved to Old Quarry South of BOUCHAVESNES and then moved again up to B/112 position. C/112 moved to position East of Canal. Bosche still retiring.	
	6th.		B.H.Q. moved to Old Quarry about 2000 yards East of MOISLAINS. Batteries moved up to positions S. of NURLU. 175th Infantry Bde 58th Div took over from 141 Bde 47th Division. Lieut JOHNSTON killed and 7 Other ranks wounded.	
	7th.		advance continued at 8.a.m. towards GUYENCOURT - Batteries moved forward to positions near SAULCOURT WOOD. B.H.Q. moved to sunken road S.E. of LIERAMONT - Quiet night.	
	8th.		Brigade comes under the orders of the 74th Div. arty and pulls out to Wagon Lines near MOISLAINS.	
	9th.		At 4.a.m. Wagon Line shelled - B/112 had 2 men killed and 1 wounded - D/112 1 killed and 3 men wounded.	
	10th & 11th		General Cleaning up.	
	12th		112th Bde came under orders of 12 Div for purposes of defence of NURLU Line.	
	13th to 15th		Brigade at Wagon Lines.	

Army Form C. 2118.

WAR DIARY
or
INTELLIGENCE-SUMMARY.
(Erase heading not required.)

112th Brigade R.F.A.

Instructions regarding War Diaries and Intelligence Summaries are contained in F. S. Regs., Part II. and the Staff Manual respectively. Title pages will be prepared in manuscript.

Place	Date	Hour	Summary of Events and Information	Remarks and references to Appendices
In the Field.	Sept 16th 1918.		"A" and "D" Batteries moved into Battle positions South of SAULCOURT.	
	17th.		B/112 and C/112 moved into action. - B.H.Q. established near GUYENCOURT.	
	18th.		Zero hour 5.20.a.m. - At 5.30.a.m. Major Evans reported enemy barrage late in coming down and absence of lights.	
	19th.		Hostile tanks reported - B. Battery warned to deal with them and to move forward - EPEHY reported also PEZIERE - B Battery moves forward S. of EPEHY and is in action at 11.30. "A" and "D" Batteries move forward in advance of "C" Battery across the railway - Major Jones, Lt Hudson, Lt Trustrum, and Lt Mead and 14 Other ranks have to go to hospital gassed. At 4.p.m. the Bosch is reported back in POPLAR TRENCH - Major Evans in close touch with the Buffs who are held up at OLD COPSE and by M.G. fire from DELISH AVENUE - "A" and "D" Batteries owing to the Infantry withdrawal have to withdraw back to E.12.d & b. respectively.	
	20th.		Quiet Day.	
	21st.		Attack resumed 5.40.a.m. 112th Bde and 62nd Bde R.F.A. put up barrage on right half of Divisional Front. "A" "B" and "D" Batteries shoot into LARK POST which is holding up our advance. At midday R.W. KENTS report enemy advancing diagonally through F.5.c.central, all batteries put down barrage 200 yards East of this line. Infantry bothered by M.G. fire from BRAETON POST TOMBOIS FARM and LITTLE PRIEL FARM, 2 guns, D Batt, 2 guns B. Batt, 1 section "C" Battery put on each respectively. at 1.15. ordered to stop shooting on LITTLE PRIEL FARM as we are about to attack at 1.25. Bosch counter attacked, but not very strongly and driven off. B.M. orders registration of Red Line by Daylight.	
	22nd.		5.30.a.m. "C" Battery fired salvos every 5 minutes on BIRDLANE - "D" Battery O.P. was very heavily shelled with Phosgine about midday.	
	23rd.		10.55.a.m. Enemy reported working down CRELLIN AVENUE - "A" and "D" Battery shoot it up. Some good targets shot on in CRELLIN AVENUE and KINGSTON QUARRY. Special night firing in view of prisoners statements that ALPINE Regt was being relieved.	

Army Form C. 2118.

WAR DIARY
or
INTELLIGENCE SUMMARY.
(Erase heading not required).

112th Brigade R.F.A.

Instructions regarding War Diaries and Intelligence Summaries are contained in F. S. Regs., Part II. and the Staff Manual respectively. Title pages will be prepared in manuscript.

Place	Date	Hour	Summary of Events and Information	Remarks and references to Appendices
In the Field.	Sept 24rd		S.O.S. went up just N. of LITTLE PRIEL FARM at 11.30.a.m. - Batteries opened fire. LITTLE PRIEL FARM and CRELLIN AVENUE kept under short bursts all day. Much traffic seen on roads in S.8.a. & b. and S.15.a.	
X	25th		"A" "B" and "D" Batteries moved forward after dusk to advanced positions N.W. of RONSSOY. "A" Battery fired 500 rounds B.B. Gas shells on HINDENBURG LINE during night.	
X	26th		5.20.a.m. S.O.S. went up - 6.5.a.m. cease fire. 112th Brigade came under orders of 4th Australian Div C.R.A. Northern group covering 27th American Division at 10.a.m.	
	27th		Attack by 27th and 30th American Divisions launched at 5.30.a.m. with object of securing line running through GILLEMONT and QUENEMONT FM. All objectives secured. "A" Battery captured 1 officer prisoner.	
	28th		All Batteries carried on Bombardment tasks on HINDENBURG LINE - During night 28th/29th Batteries moved into action E. of RONSSOY, under heavy shell and M.G. Fire.	
	29th		attack by 27th and 30th American Divisions, 3rd and 5th Australian Divisions to pass through attack launched at 5.30.a.m. - Situation very obscure during day.	
	30th		At 5.30.p.m. 112th Brigade R.F.A. withdrew to Wagon Lines into Divisional Mobile Reserve. South of EPEHY.	

Commanding 112th Brigade R.F.A.   Lieut. Col. R.F.A.

Army Form C. 2118.

WAR DIARY
or
INTELLIGENCE SUMMARY

(Erase heading not required.)

112th Brigade R.F.A.

Place	Date	Hour	Summary of Events and Information	Remarks and references to Appendices
In the Field	Oct 1st 1918		Batteries in action near KNOLL behind BONY for attack on GOUY Line.	
	2nd.		Batteries in action near KNOLL behind BONY - Exposed to heavy shell and M.G. fire and casualties.	
	3rd.		Batteries withdrawn to W.L. E.12.b. near EPEHY.	
	4th		Resting in W.L.	
	5th		Batteries were ordered to move into action near BELLICOURT and B.H.Q. moved to HINDENBURG LINE near BONY - Orders cancelled and Batteries bivouaced for night near HARGICOURT.	
	6th		Brigade moved into Battery positions at CABARET WOOD COPSE for attack on BEAUREVOIR.	
	7th		Brigade moved to positions by Quarry behind BEAUREVOIR.	
	8th		Brigade fired barrage for attack on AUDIGNY line and advanced to positions between SERAIN and BEAUREVOIR.	
	9th		Attack proceeding, and Cavalry attacked HONNECHY. The Brigade moved up towards MARETZ and remained in readiness near MARCH COPSE. B.H.Q. moved to TROU AUX SOLDATS. Brigade at HONNECHY.	
	10th		Batteries rendezvous - and moved into action behind ESCAUFORT. Brigade at HONNECHY.	
	11th to 16th		In action behind ESCAUFORT. Brigade at HONNECHY.	
	17th		Attack on SELLE. "A" Battery advanced others remained.	
	18th		Batteries advanced over railway to behind BASUEL - Brigade at ST BENIN.	

Army Form C. 2118.

WAR DIARY
or
INTELLIGENCE-SUMMARY.   112th Brigade R.F.A.
(Erase heading not required.)

Instructions regarding War Diaries and Intelligence Summaries are contained in F. S. Regs., Part II. and the Staff Manual respectively. Title pages will be prepared in manuscript.

Place	Date	Hour	Summary of Events and Information	Remarks and references to Appendices
In the Field	Oct 19th to 23rd.		Batteries in action behind BASUEL - Brigade at ST BENIN.	
	24th		Attack on POMMEREUIL - Batteries moved into action near LE CATEAU and then near FME DES TILLEULS near BOIS D EVEQUE - Brigade at POMMEREUIL.	
	25th & 26th		Batteries in action near BOIS D EVEQUE - Brigade at POMMEREUIL.	
	27th		Brigade relieved by 66th D.A. and came out to rest at HONNECHY.	
	28th to 31st		Brigade resting at HONNECHY. Reconnoitred positions behind MALGARNI.	

Major R.F.A.
Commanding 112th Brigade R.F.A.

Army Form C. 2118.

WAR DIARY
or
INTELLIGENCE SUMMARY.

112th BRIGADE. R.F.A.

(Erase heading not required.)

Place	Date	Hour	Summary of Events and Information	Remarks and references to Appendices
In the Field.	Nov. 1st.		Brigade at rest in HONNECHY.	
	2nd.		Batteries moved into action on East of BOIS L'EVEQUE. Brigade H.Qrs at POMMEREUIL.	
	3rd.		Digging in and completing Ammunition supply.	
	4th.		Attack on LANDRECIES launched at Zero hour. advanced Brigade H.Qrs established at MALGARNI. 2nd.Lieut.Padley went forward as F.O.O but was killed on way out. Attack successful & All btys moved forward to HAUT CORNEE during afternoon, Bde Hqtrs. established in liaison with 75th Bde Inf, at HAPPEGARBE.	
	5th		Bde rested in action.	
	6th		Bde marched to MAROILLES and billeted there for the night.	
	7th.		Advance continued 112th Bde working under orders G.O.C. 75 Inf Bde C/112 and 2 Hows D/112 attached to 1/5 th Gloucesters. During afternoon all batteries moved into action East of MARBAIX, Bde Hqtrs at DOMPIERRE	
	8th		Advance continued at close of day all batteries in action N E of AVESNES.	
	9th		112th Bde relieved by 331 Bde and marched to LANDRECIES.	
	10th		Cleaning up	
	11th		Armistice Day.	
	12th		Cleaning up etc.	
	13th		-do-	
	14th		Bde moved to St Benin,	
	15th		Salvage operations commenced.	

Army Form C. 2118.

WAR DIARY
or
INTELLIGENCE SUMMARY.
(Erase heading not required.)

Instructions regarding War Diaries and Intelligence Summaries are contained in F. S. Regs., Part II. and the Staff Manual respectively. Title pages will be prepared in manuscript.

Place	Date	Hour	Summary of Events and Information	Remarks and references to Appendices
In the Field.	16th		Salvage operations.	
	17th		-do-	
	18th		-do-	
	19th		-do-	
	20th		-do-	
	21st		-do-	
	22nd		-do-	
	23rd		-do-	
	24th		-do-	
	25th		-do-	
	26th		-do-	
	27th		-do-	
	28th		-do-	
	29th		-do-	
	30th		Bde moved to CARNIERES and formed part of 75th Inf Bde group, salvage operations continued.	

Major R.F.A.
Commanding 112th Brigade R.F.A.

Army Form C. 2118.

WAR DIARY
or
INTELLIGENCE SUMMARY.

112th Brigade R.F.A.

(Erase heading not required.)

Instructions regarding War Diaries and Intelligence Summaries are contained in F. S. Regs., Part II. and the Staff Manual respectively. Title pages will be prepared in manuscript.

Place	Date	Hour	Summary of Events and Information	Remarks and references to Appendices
In the Field.	Dec. 1st.		Salvage Operation continued.	
	2nd.		-do- -do-	
	3rd.		-do- -do-	
	4th.		His Majesty the King visited the Village the Brigade lined part of route, all salvage operation suspended.	
	5th		Salvage operations resumed.	
	6th to 31st.		Salvage operation and recreation carried on.	
	1.1.19			

L.H.Menzies Lt. Col. R.F.A.
Commanding 112th Brigade R.F.A.

Army Form C. 2118.

112th Brigade R.F.A.

Vol 39

WAR DIARY
or
INTELLIGENCE-SUMMARY.
(Erase heading not required.)

Instructions regarding War Diaries and Intelligence Summaries are contained in F. S. Regs., Part II. and the Staff Manual respectively. Title pages will be prepared in manuscript.

Place	Date	Hour	Summary of Events and Information	Remarks and references to Appendices
In the field	Jan 1st to 31st		At Carnieres. Salvage Operations carried on, all possibel assistance rendered to Civilians, and Field Service Marching Order Parades held each week.	
	1.2.19.			

JHCurzon
Lieut Col R.F.A.
Commanding 112th Brigade R.F.A.

Army Form C. 2118.

WAR DIARY
or
INTELLIGENCE SUMMARY
112th Brigade R.F.A.

(Erase heading not required.)

Instructions regarding War Diaries and Intelligence Summaries are contained in F. S. Regs., Part II. and the Staff Manual respectively. Title pages will be prepared in manuscript.

Place	Date	Hour	Summary of Events and Information	Remarks and references to Appendices
CARNIERES NORD.	Feb. 1st to 28th.		At Carnieres. Salvage Operations carried on, all possible assistance rendered to Civilians. Parades and Field Service Marching Order held each week.	
			28.2.19.	
			[signature] Lieut-Col R.F.A. Commanding 112th Brigade. R.F.A.	

www.ingramcontent.com/pod-product-compliance
Lightning Source LLC
Chambersburg PA
CBHW081403160426
43193CB00013B/2096